When A
Child Dies

Carol Pregent

When A Child Dies

AVE MARIA PRESS
Notre Dame, Indiana 46556

Contents

Foreword 7

ONE
Death 9

TWO
People 17

THREE
Funeral 25

FOUR
Grief 31

FIVE
God 39

SIX
Memories 45

SEVEN
Life 53

EIGHT
Pieces 59

NINE
Faith 67

TEN
Hope 75

ELEVEN
Love 83

TWELVE
Prayer 91

THIRTEEN
Help 99

FOURTEEEN
Suggestions 111

Epilogue 115

Foreword

While seeking to be healed from the physical, emotional, and spiritual pain of grief, I realized that sharing with other grieving parents was helpful. This is the story of my pain, of my work through grief. I offer it to you with all the love in my heart, hoping to help you in your struggle with grief. I also offer my story in response to a gentle nudge from divine inspiration. I believe that I am connected to you, and you to me, somehow, in this fellowship of suffering; and I pray for all grieving mothers everywhere as we struggle to find our way to wholeness which is God.

ONE

Death

My days were limited before one of them existed.
—Psalm 139:16 (*NAB*)

She tossed and turned in her bed. Her head moved up and down, back and forth in an effort to breathe. She seemed more than restless, perhaps annoyed or irritated. One word escaped her lips in a gasp, "Oxygen." "Mom's coming, Lisa," I answered, moving my tired body out of the comfortable reclining chair. "It's going to be a long night," I thought to myself. I opened the tank, adjusted the flow meter, and handed my daughter the plastic nose piece. This tank was very low, but there was a spare under her bed. Checking the small, silver cylinder, I wondered how long the supply would last. "Turn over this way, Lisa, toward me," I said. "No mom, no I don't want to," was her answer. "Oh, just for a short while," I said while already turning her tiny frame. "You've been facing that way all evening." Getting the lotion out, I started to rub her bony hip where a large red circle seemed like a permanent mark.

9

This was the child I carried, my first born. "O Lord God," I prayed, "help us through the night." She looked so small and fragile lying in her bed, more like ten years old than seventeen. Her body had wasted away these past six weeks of being bedridden. That womanly seventeen-year-old figure had turned into skin and bones, toothpick legs, skeleton arms, bony shoulders and hips. Was this really my baby? O God, help me! Her beautiful cover-girl face, olive skin, rosy cheeks, smiling impish grin, and twinkling hazel eyes were but lovely memories now, replaced with a chilling grayish color; no smile, no twinkle, just a shadow of death. She was such a vivacious girl, full of life, bubbling over, effervescent. And now, her labored breathing filled the room.

I sat on the edge of her bed and, rubbing lotion on her legs, I looked around her bedroom. This beautiful room that I had always loved—the purple room as we called it, designed for Lisa—had now become the hub of our entire household. The smallish, sunken room, actually a garage loft, was a teenager's dream, Lisa often said. The deep purple carpeting, Lisa's favorite color since she was five, and daintily flowered wallpaper presented a girlish mood. The room held three large closets, perfect for a teenage girl, and double french doors opening onto a private veranda. Included among the furnishings were a lavender book case, Lisa loved to read—everything from Shakespeare to Agatha Christie to modern romance—and a small lavender desk, rarely used for homework. Lisa rarely did homework. There was also a solid maple powder table—her eighth grade graduation present— loaded with all the latest cosmetics, fragrances, and beauty aids. This room held life, vibrant young life.

"More oxygen, mom," said Lisa. I rolled the spare cylinder out from under her bed just as her father came into the room. Dennis—my husband, my lover, my support— looked so tired and worried. I wondered if I looked that way, too. He cracked the spare oxygen tank, set it up, then immediately left to call the supply house. It was after midnight, but a respiratory therapist was on call twenty-four hours.

Lisa's breathing was gurgling and bubbling; one lung had collapsed a month ago and she was breathing on part of the other. Yet, we still had no indication that this would be her final night. This night seemed like so many others. I hoped that we could get some sleep soon. Maybe after the oxygen was delivered we could all settle down, Dennis on the floor by Lisa's bed, and me in the reclining chair. Lisa was still restless, but very quiet tonight.

My mind wandered off to our last shopping trip, Lisa and I. What fun we had! We were two girls together with money to spend and we laughed and chatted gaily. All the focus was on Lisa and she was at her best, smiling and chattering as she tried on outfit after outfit. It was so good to be with her. She was beautiful and life-giving. I ignored the fact that she was pale and very thin. After purchasing three or four tops with slacks to match, we stopped to have a sandwich. Lisa looked tired, and thoughts of her illness came to mind. Our sandwiches and fries came, and I pushed away the disturbing thoughts. But just the smell of the hot steaming roast beef sandwich made Lisa sick to her stomach, and she pushed away the food. I began to cry. Lisa pleaded, "Please don't, mom. We've had such a fun shopping trip; don't spoil it now."

The clang of metal interrupted my thoughts as the oxygen arrived. I frowned at the large, ugly, dark green tank—another symbol of desecration clashing into our lavender sanctuary. "I've got another one to bring up," he said. "Fine," I said, but it was not at all fine. I hated the sight of it but I couldn't hide it away, as I had the portable potty, bedpan, and other landmarks of defeat. Well now, there they were in place, large and slightly rusty green against the lavender and pink flowered wallpaper. "Would you listen to her lungs?" I asked the respiratory therapist. He seemed eager enough to listen, but less eager to explain to us. He appeared to be nervous or at least uncomfortable. He mumbled something about usually working with old people. Yes, I thought to myself, "What a shock to see death embracing youth," looking at my daughter and still not realizing that this night would be her last.

As I looked around to assess the situation, I realized how very tired I was. It was now the early hours of the morning on Saturday the seventh of March. This would be the day of my child's death. Lisa remained very quiet and detached. She lay still with her eyes closed and could have been drifting in and out of sleep. At any rate, she was not communicating with us. "We might as well get some much-needed sleep," I said to my husband. He laid on the floor beside Lisa's bed with his pillow and blanket and quickly fell asleep. I went to the hall closet for a comforter, and then snuggled into the large reclining chair that we had purchased just for this purpose, to keep the night watch. I had hardly made myself comfortable, when Lisa rather urgently cried out, to no one in particular, "Quick, I need oxygen, quick, quick!" Up out of the cozy chair again, I was quickly at her bedside. While I fumbled with the new oxygen tanks, I called across the room to awaken Dennis. He came to the other side of Lisa's bed and, sensing how upset I was, he untwisted the plastic cording and placed the nose piece on Lisa. Then we sat, each on one side of her bed. Lisa's thin frame barely caused a bump in the blanket between us.

We looked at each other, Dennis and I, our eyes filled with questions. I saw no answers in his, and I knew he saw none in mine. What was happening to us? What was happening to our baby? We had been through so much; she had been through so much. I remember the exact day that Lisa told me of "the intruder" in our life. Sitting side by side at our long dining room table, she said to me, "Mom, my throat feels lumpy, and it hurts when I play the trombone." "Oh Lisa," I answered, "I'll bet you have strep throat." It was in October, a crisp, sunny day, late in the afternoon. Lisa had been busy for weeks practicing with the high school band. They played at the football game every Friday, and usually had a band contest on Saturday. This, coupled with practices during the week, late nights to bed, and early mornings up, would make anyone run down, I reasoned. "You know, Lisa," I said, "you've been keeping crazy hours and not eating properly either. You also look like you've lost some weight." I began with the basic principles of caring for your body and then quickly moved into a full mothering lecture on proper rest and nutrition.

The next two weeks were confusing and seem hazy to recall. There were the penicillin pills that Dennis brought home from his physician for Lisa's "strep throat." I now became very aware of her lack of appetite. Then I found the diet pills in her purse quite by accident, and that same night she showed me a lump near her collar bone. I kept Lisa out of school for the next two days, and took her to the family doctor that Saturday.

Dennis, once again, was adjusting the oxygen tube on Lisa's ashen face. She was restless and her head moved back and forth. She would snatch the oxygen tubing from her face and throw it down. Then, seconds later came her shallow cry, "Oxygen, quick!" Oh, how I wanted her to talk to me, but there was no verbal exchange. Lisa maintained a distant dreamy quality that was hard to put my finger on . . . a kind of detachment, suspension. Did she realize that she hovered between life and death? We did not realize it yet.

It was now the early hours of morning. I was so very tired that I laid down in bed beside my daughter. She was turned away from me facing her father who sat in a chair on the other side of the bed. I rubbed her back and she moaned a little, so I continued to rub her back. She never focused her eyes on me again. She never spoke to me again. I can't even remember the last words she said to me. Dennis held the oxygen tube in his hands for a long time. Her shallow breathing continued.

My mind kept drifting back through time and I went over and over the events that led us here. The year or so of chemotherapy was long, frightening, and unpredictable; and Lisa fought it every inch of the way. Every other week the drive to Children's Hospital was tense and filled with anxiety. Many weeks Lisa begged not to go—couldn't we skip it or at least put it off? She slipped from young woman to small child and back again repeatedly. Some weeks she staunchly refused treatment, and we threatened and bribed and pleaded. On the return trip home she would be totally broken—violently ill and crying, a limp bundle of vomit and tears huddled in a corner of the van, while I drove the forty-five minutes to our home. My mother's heart was twisted and torn.

And so the year inched by, one sick week, one good week, and much pain for all. As spring came, the school year finally ended, and then we went on to radiation treatments. These were every day, but in a different hospital. It was still a forty-five minute drive, but now a new doctor, new staff, etc. And so we continued throughout the summer. The bonus was that these treatments did not cause Lisa to be violently ill. And she and I often joked about how easy this was. "A piece of cake," we quipped. "Why, we could do this standing on our heads." "We're on the downhill side." "Nothing to it." "Easy street."

And finally the last day came. Lisa was bubbling with excitement and she even "dressed" for the occasion. Just enough of her hair had grown back so that she had a very, very short but stylish hairdo. She wore a white, full-skirted sundress with big, white earrings and a big, wide smile. She looked so beautiful and it was easy to tell that she felt good and so proud of herself. I was proud of her, too—it had been a hard year, but she made it. We made it together. This was "graduation day." She went to treatment this last time with her close friend, Ricky. They were both excited and glad to be together for the "grand finale." They even took along Lisa's sisters, whom Lisa had carefully outfitted in ruffly sundresses for the special occasion. And so the small party departed in Ricky's old car with an exhilarating air about them.

I could not quite identify my feelings. At best I was cautiously optimistic. Trying to sort things out in my mind,

I prayed, "Thank you, God, for taking care of my daughter."

My husband's voice brought me back to the reality of the moment. "Her eyes," he said, "her eyes look funny, something's wrong, very wrong." There was a tinge of fear in his masculine voice. I was still lying in Lisa's bed and she had her back to me. I couldn't see her face, but I sensed what was happening. I knew in my heart at that moment that Lisa's meeting with death had begun. I didn't answer Dennis, though I saw his anxious face, and his eyes questioning me, "She isn't going to die now, is she? Say it isn't so." I closed my eyes and laid my head on Lisa's pillow, beside her head. I tried to pray, or at least I wanted to, but no prayers would come. I tried to think of a scripture verse, something I could prayerfully repeat to myself, something to hold on to. Nothing came. I couldn't think or pray. I was suspended in this valley of the shadow of death, unable to come up with anything in my human mind to support me.

I lay still, beside my child, who seemed to be engaged in a restless struggle with the inevitable thing that was happening to her, overcoming her, overpowering her. She was restless and disturbed. Seemingly out of the depths of her being, came a rattling, raspy, whisper of a word in a voice I didn't recognize, "D—a—d." Ever so slowly it escaped her lips. "I'm right here, Lisa," answered her father. "We are right beside you. We will stay with you." And once again, with more urgency and slightly louder, she said, "D—a—d." "Don't be afraid. We are with you," repeated Dennis. And yet her mouth moved in an effort to communicate with only silent words escaping. Once again in a strange and haunting whisper, "Dad." What a struggle for her to say that word. It seemed to take every ounce of strength that she could command. And still, she seemed to want to communicate something which she no longer had the capacity to do. My heart felt like a wet dishrag that had been wrung dry. Dad was the last word Lisa said. She said it quite a few times—maybe five, maybe seven—I'm not sure. It was such a struggle for her to speak each time; but she seemed to be overcome with the need to say something. Something that will forever remain unspoken.

Finally, when words no longer came, she stopped trying to speak, but she continued to struggle with something. She remained restless and sighed deeply. I rubbed her back softly, ever so gently, my baby, my first born. "It's all right, Lisa," I whispered. "Just let go, it will be all right." Dennis looked at me with panic in his eyes. I continued, "It's OK, Lisa, let yourself go, it will be so beautiful when you get there. It will be wonderful, so wonderful we can't even imagine! You can do it—you can make it—it will be good— just let go." She heaved a great sigh and her body relaxed. The struggling stopped. Dennis looked at me "Is she . . . is she . . . ?" "No, she's not dead, and I know she can hear us," I whispered. He began, "Lisa, we love you, we love you and we'll stay right here beside you." "Lisa," I said, "do you believe that it's going to be wonderful when you get there?" She nodded her head twice.

I got up out of her bed and moved to the opposite side near Dennis. Now I could see her face and I realized what my husband was feeling. Her eyes were open, but unfocused in a distant stare. Mucous strands had formed from the eyelid to the bottom eyelashes. I quickly took a tissue from her end table and tried to wipe away the mucous. But even as I touched her eye, she did not blink, and I immediately withdrew my hand. Her face was grayish color, and mucous had also formed in and around her mouth. Yet she was still faintly, quietly breathing.

Dennis left the room to call the hospice nurse who had been caring for Lisa for the past month or so. When he returned, he sat on the edge of her bed, and Lisa rolled over on her back with her head resting in his lap. It was there that she died, with Dennis holding her in his arms. She took four or five last breaths, deep rattling breaths, with long spaces in between. After each breath her body collapsed, and Dennis and I looked at each other, wondering if that was the end. Then, after what seemed like a very long space of time, another rattling breath came. Finally, no more breaths came.

TWO

People

Blessed are the merciful for they will be shown mercy.
—Matthew 5:7 (*NAB*)

March 7, 1987 was a bright and sunny Saturday morning. It was an early spring day, breezy and warm, as I stood on the side porch in my nightgown and sweater and watched the hearse depart. My mind was thinking, "I guess I won't get to be the mother of the bride." My hope for the future was leaving in that hearse. My husband gently guided me indoors. I was numb. I was thinking but not thinking, feeling but not feeling. I was unable to focus entirely on the magnitude of what had just happened. From the moment I had heard the nurse on the phone say, "Doctor, Lisa Pregent has expired," my mind became soggy. It seemed as though I was taking in knowledge, but unable to fully grasp it or hold it in my head for long.

Earlier, looking at my daughter's lifeless body lying in her bed, the scripture came to me, "Rachel wails for her

children because they are no more." And once again, being
accustomed to praying, I wanted to pray, but nothing came.
I threw myself across Lisa's bed and sobbed uncontrollably.
Her small, still body motionless under me, our two bodies
formed the cross. And even as I sobbed, my mind darted
about—"Wails for her children because they are no more . . .
O my God, I can't believe this is happening . . . this is the little
girl I carried."And then, peeking through the window curtains, I saw the hearse pull up. I wanted the world to stand
still, the moment to stop, so I could try to get a hold on what
was happening, but the scene continued to unfold. There was
Dennis, carrying Lisa's body down the steps and toward that
narrow stretcher. And then I saw the other people, the nurse
quickly leaving out the side door. Where was she going and
why was she leaving at a time like this? Then there were those
two men, dressed in suits so nicely, looking so business-like.
They just stood off to the side as we walked in slow motion
carrying our child. They didn't seem to take charge; it seemed
as though *we* were in charge. "Help us," I thought, "we don't
know what to do!"

My husband put our child's body on the stretcher, and I
noticed my girlfriend standing on the other side of the
stretcher. "When did you get here?" I thought, "How did you
know?" But she didn't look at me. She looked frightened and
stared at Lisa's body. I wondered why she was frightened.
Then I held my child and cried. My mind kept repeating the
verse about wailing for her children, and it also wished that
the people would go away, especially the two men behind
me waiting to take my child. And then they were gone.

Rose was frightened. That's why she looked it. She hadn't
seen death before and that was her reaction. She had been my
closest friend and companion throughout Lisa's illness. She
was a faithful friend, someone I knew I could trust. Now, she
hurried across the street to tell my neighbor the news. As I
watched Rose returning with Martha, I thought about how
much those two women had helped me make it through
many hard days. They were both steady-eddies, willing to

help in any way. Good women. Now they listened as I recounted all the events of our walk through the shadow of death. At first it seemed as though I was talking about other people instead of us. It felt like such unfamiliar territory, it hardly seemed real. I think I told them the whole story more than once, and repeated myself many times on different parts. This was just the beginning of my repeating the story many times. It seemed I couldn't stop myself even if I wanted to. I incessantly relived the night again and again all day, and in days to come.

That morning, my thoughts quickly turned to my other children who had spent the night with gramma and grampa. Now all at once, they were back, and I felt so unprepared to talk to them. I gathered them together and spoke softly, "Lisa died." The words were hardly out of my mouth when my now oldest child stomped up the stairs. Not believing my words, she headed for Lisa's room. Two others held on to me crying, and another went quietly to her room. I had read everything I could find about death, but I was not prepared for this day—I don't think I could have been. I stood helpless and hurting within myself, not having any idea how to help my children.

Meanwhile, the funeral director was back, a kindly old gentleman still in his business suit, asking all sorts of questions. I sat there, in my night dress, listening to my husband talk with him. What would the obituary read? What would Lisa wear? Such questions at a time like this. My mind couldn't function in all these directions yet. Lisa and I had discussed the issue of what she would wear: red dress . . . band uniform . . . prom gown. It seemed more real at that time than it did now. We supplied whatever information we could think of, but we just couldn't think properly.

There were three days between the death and the funeral. Those three days were hazy and confusing at best. We saw and talked to more people than we had in years. I was at my worst, and most vulnerable. Nothing made sense. There were lots of people in our home at all times—friends, neighbors, relatives, children. Throughout all the haze and confusion, I could see everything in a different light, a new vision, as it were, looking at things in light of death. The people seemed to have so much more worth. There really was a deeper meaning in relationships, much more reason to cling to each other. People were more valuable than I had seemed to know; and I wondered why I hadn't seen that before.

At some point during the afternoon, we went to the funeral home to take care of the business of selecting and organizing. The same two men in business suits helped us through. One old and one young, grandfather and grandson. They were both soft-spoken and very gracious. In fact, this was the most non-threatening and most comforting conversation in my memory. They seemed to want to do exactly whatever we needed them to do. They seemed totally open and willing to serve us in any way they could. Again the value of people was impressed upon me.

From there we traveled to the cemetery to purchase a final resting place. It was late afternoon by now. The sky had clouded over and a brisk wind blew across the graveyard as our van drove up the road. I was still having trouble in my mind trying to link the chain of events together. I could not fully grasp what had happened. Occasionally, glimpses of the reality of the situation shivered through me and I broke down in wrenching sobs. But these times were interspersed with unexplainable disbelief and empty thoughts totally unrelated to the situation. I was beginning to think that I might be losing my mind.

We arrived at the custodian's office in the cemetery. I don't remember what he looked like except that he was bearded. I do remember that he was helpful and cautiously friendly, choosing his words rather carefully it seemed, lest he offend us. He unrolled a large topographical map of the graveyard and pointed to different areas and specific plots that might be suitable. Dennis asked him to come with us in our van to view the plots. I could tell that he didn't want to, but he did, grabbing his shovel "to mark out the grave." We drove to a few different sites. Finally Dennis stopped the van. His mind also seemed muddled as he thought aloud trying to decide. My mind was on overload and my feelings were raw. "Let's just pick a spot and get out of here," I screamed in my thoughts. Dennis was asking the custodian, "If it were your child, which place would you choose?" Now it was obvious he was really uncomfortable. "I've never thought about that," he answered. "Neither have we," said Dennis, "until now. Could you think about it and help us decide?" And so he thought for a minute or two, then answered, "I would pick that higher spot up there." And so we paid for that spot and left, without even trying to grasp the significance of what had transpired.

We slowly drove back to our home, which by now was quite full of people. I had an overwhelming desire to be with my mother, who had not yet arrived from a distant state. On the drive back from the cemetery, my thoughts turned toward mom. It certainly seemed very strange to me as our family was just an ordinary family, not exceptionally close or even outwardly affectionate. All the same, I wanted my mother. I wanted to slip back into the role of child, to be mothered, to have her put her arms around me and say, "There, there, go ahead and cry. That's all right. Let it all out."

As our van pulled up to the curb, my friend Peggy walked toward me with compassion written all over her face. A widow herself, her husband had died of cancer a few years before. She had met death and she understood how I felt. She held me in her arms and all the pent up emotion spilled out in sobs once again. "It hurts. I know," she said. "It's all right. Let it out." I wanted her to hold me forever. Maybe then I could escape the pain that pressed in on me from all sides. Peg and I had talked many times about pain and hurting inside. She had jokingly used the expression, "putting on my big girl dress," which meant to face the realities of life even when we didn't want to. And as I cried and she comforted me, I knew I would have to "put on my big girl dress," but I didn't want to.

Our house seemed to have a lot of activity going on. I

couldn't sort it out, nor did I care to. Lisa's friends came in and out. A small group clustered in her bedroom. Our children's friends were in and out, and our neighbors stopped by to drop off food or just to see if they could help in any way. Dennis' family was busy caring for our children, answering the phone and door, and managing the household. Other friends and neighbors were also helping with the busyness of life. Everyone seemed to want to be for us.

People in our lives at this time seemed to also have some difficulty dealing with what happened to us. The people who came forward to help us were uncertain, unsure of what to say or do, but wanting to help anyway. Some just sat and listened and let me retell my story over and over. Others cooked, cleaned, brought food, transported my children to and from school, ironed, ran errands, rocked my fussy baby, answered the phone, did the laundry. Someone bought our son a jacket. Another person bought two of our children new shoes, and I wasn't even aware that they needed them. It was surprising to me who some of the people were, but their overwhelming care and concern for us at this time restored my faith in humanity.

There were some people who avoided us, probably because they just couldn't handle the situation and didn't know what to say or do. And so they did nothing. I could understand this, but I didn't have the strength or the will to do anything about it. I lost some relationships that had meant a lot to me, but I seemed powerless to make an effort at picking up the pieces.

What can I say about all these people? I didn't want them around me, but I didn't want them to leave. I wanted to be alone, but it was comforting to have people around. I didn't want to be loved, and they loved me anyway. I could have never made it through this far without them.

The calling hours were five to eight, one time only. She looked beautiful, lying there in her full length prom gown, new hairdo, make-up on. She looked more beautiful in death than she had the last months of life. The children were confused. They were sure they had seen her move. They were certain she must be alive. Dennis patiently explained, "This is the bed that Lisa's body will rest in. This is only her body. Lisa's spirit is in heaven with Jesus." "But daddy," the little ones said, "I think she is only sleeping." I tried to help. "Now listen," I said, "this part of Lisa here is the body that she used while she was on earth. The other part of Lisa, the part that laughed and cried and loved us, that part has gone up to heaven and so she doesn't need this body, and we will see her again when we get there." "We want to go now," they answered.

They looked her all over and looked at all the flowers, and so did I. I could tell they were confused and could not grasp the full meaning, and neither could I. I could tell that they were hurt and angry, and so was I. I could see that their little minds just plainly did not know what to do with this information, and neither did mine.

Many people came and went. I lost track of where my children were, but every now and then one would rush over to the casket and touch her body. Our now oldest child seemed to stay the farthest away. Most of the time she spent in the foyer watching people coming and going. Our only son, three years old, stayed closest to the casket. Lisa had always called him her buddy. He kept repeating, "My buddy died." It was a hard night's work. We left feeling empty and exhausted, but thankful that the people cared enough to come. "O my God, thank you for the people. Please, let me never forget to be thankful for people."

THREE

Funeral

A grain of wheat remains no more than a single grain unless it is dropped into the ground and dies. If it does die, then it produces many grains.

—John 12:24

The morning of the funeral arrived, bitter cold and windy. "How appropriate," I thought, "a bitter day for a bitter task." My mind kept "singing" the words, "This is the little girl I carried," in a mournful lament. What a strange feeling I had this day. I felt removed from the situation, like I was watching things happen. The funeral mass was scheduled for 10:30 a.m. Lisa and I had talked about this service at length, several times. "If I die," said Lisa, "let's have a wonderfully elaborate funeral! We could have the whole school band play in church! It'd be great!" "Oh," I said, "it probably wouldn't be elaborate, Lisa. You know how I like simple." But, "It's *my* funeral," she teased, "so you *have* to do it *my* way." And then there was the day she said, "Mom, let's figure out who the

pall bearers will be." "OK Lisa, who do you think?" "Well,"
she began, "Ricky, definitely Ricky . . . and Dave . . . also Doug
. . . write them down, mom, OK—so you'll remember." I got
a piece of paper and wrote them down. "How hard it is to be
a mother," I thought. "And oh yes!" said Lisa, "we've just *got*
to sing 'City of God.' I just love that song!"

Now the day was upon us, and I was behaving in a
manner befitting the situation. Seemingly mindless, I con-
ducted myself through the motions of the day wondering at
every step, "How is this happening? How could this be true?
My life is at a crossroad, my child is dead, and my God is
silent. Will I make it through this day? Please may I lie down
and die also?"

Once again we came to the funeral home. There she lay
in the same spot, a vision of beauty—sleeping beauty to be
sure. The sight of her in that full-length prom gown took my
breath away. I touched her cold, hard arm, "Lisa, can you see
me? Lisa can you hear me? Exactly what is happening where
you are? I want to know." My little ones were placing pictures
in her casket that they had drawn last night. I looked at the
carefully crayoned stick figure crying. Large tears were
placed in a line from round eyes, past a frowning mouth, past
lines that looked like empty arms held out, and on down to
the bottom of the paper. Another stick figure, this one with
wings and long flowing hair, floated at the top of the paper.

More people were coming into the room, some I hadn't
seen last night, or didn't remember. I don't know which. I sat
down and watched what was happening, feeling like an
innocent bystander, or a survivor who didn't want to be a
survivor. My heart was heavily laden with an overpowering
feeling I had never experienced. My arms and legs weighed
at least fifty pounds apiece. It seemed difficult to hold up my
body, and I had to exert great strength and an act of my will
to simply sit in the chair or stand up.

Lisa's best girlfriend, Anne, arrived carrying her Raggedy Ann doll. We also had brought with us Lisa's Raggedy
Ann. She had received it as a gift when she was born. She

slept with it every night for quite a few years before it became old and tattered. I had tried to coax her into sleeping with another toy. I even bribed her with expensive stuffed animals, plush and soft. But she clung to Raggedy Ann and hugged her in her sleep every night, even when she was old enough not to want her friends to know it. And now, Anne tucked the two rag dolls in the crook of Lisa's arms, one on each side. How pathetic they looked, soiled and worn, tattered and torn. It was plain to see that they had lived long enough and deserved to be at the end of their life.

The thought came to me to tuck Lisa in bed for the very last time. I moved toward the casket, conscious of the people behind me and wishing that we were alone in this room, mother and child, these two bodies touching for the last time ever. There was a piece of white cloth rolled at the bottom near her feet. I pulled it up over her body—past the little white heels clean and new that would never be walked on, past the floor-length taffeta skirt puffy with under flounces, past her tiny hands in lacy white gloves, past the crayoned drawings and the worn out rag dolls, and I tucked it under her chin.

I wanted to be the last person to leave the room, but we were called to leave first. Glancing back for one last look at my sleeping princess, I saw a single flower in a vase with a helium balloon attached. The funeral director brought it to me and I had one of my little ones hold it as we left to get into the car. We were in a limousine. Dennis sat in the front seat with our young son, the girls and I sat in back. My little one still held the helium balloon. People began coming out of the funeral home and getting into cars. There was mom. She looked so thin and frail but still pretty as ever in a dark green dress. She was sobbing now, my sister supporting her. "Where was dad?" I thought, but I couldn't look for him. I watched my mother walk to the car—pale and fragile. She looked as though she would be blown away in a gust of wind were it not for my sister holding her up. Everyone walked past our car as we waited to start the procession. Slowly we inched the half mile or so to the church. This seemed like a slow motion movie, made before sound. I was unsure of the script; but, yes, I had a part, and somehow I kept moving in the right direction.

We processed into the church, behind the casket carrying the still form of my oldest child. My heart was broken, half of it in the casket, half of it on the altar as we stood in the back of the church. The priest and the altar servers carrying candles walked down the aisle to meet us. The priest was an older gray-haired man whom Lisa loved. He had been her friend and confidant in her struggle. The altar servers were a girlfriend's boys, and it was a comfort to see them, but I don't know why. It was a comfort just seeing so many people—some I didn't even recognize.

"Amazing grace, how sweet the sound, that saved a wretch like me . . ." Up the aisle we processed through a sea of faces and eyes, all blurring into one large picture. Seated in our assigned pew, I was worn out, empty, and unable to string two thoughts together. Looking to my right I could see the casket in the middle aisle, to my left my husband, whose face wore the effects of continued stress. Our children were seated around us. I wanted to sing and cry and scream and die. I wanted to run out of the church, but at the same time, I wanted to stay there forever. I wanted this funeral to be over and I wished it would never end. The liturgy continued and the feeling of emptiness shrouded me. Familiar voices sang familiar hymns and familiar voices read familiar scriptures. And then it was over—so soon—and finally. Voices sang, "Receive her soul and present her to God, to God the Most High."

We walked out of church, our family pushing her casket ahead of us, leaving church together for the last time. One of our little ones rested her head on the casket sobbing loudly as we walked. Another held my hand and acted brave and strong. Our little son skipped down the aisle, ducking under the casket and out the other side. We clung to each other. The band did not play, Lisa, but we did sing

"City of God" at your request.

"Will we ever get there?" I thought as we drove through the cemetery in the black limousine. More slow motion footage. "I can hardly keep up with this script. It is too painful to endure." We pulled up to our little plot with its gaping hole. Everything was covered over neatly; no pile of dirt was evident. There seemed to be hardly a trace left to boldly testify that we would soon put this tiny body into that deep, dark hole in the ground. Spring had turned to winter this cold March day, in silent affirmation of this cold final ritual. A short prayer was said, a short scripture read—and it was finished.

I didn't want to leave the cemetery, I wanted to stay in this spot at least until I could figure out if this were really true, and if so, how I could live through it. My feet seemed glued in place, my body heavy, my mind numb. My daughter let the helium balloon go, and it floated quickly upward. The priest leaned over and said to me, "No one will leave until you do." We left in the black limo, driving at a somewhat quicker pace. As we transferred our grieving family into our van, my heart and mind seemed to be back in the graveyard. It was all over too quickly. "We had left too soon," I thought. "I want to go back to the cemetery, honey," I said to my husband. "All right, we'll go back," he answered, so quickly and decisively that I knew he felt the same.

The children were quiet as we entered the cemetery for the second time, and we welcomed the silence. Up a hill, around the first curve, one more curve, and we were at the top of a knoll looking down on the grave site. The casket stood poised above the grave. There were several teenage girls holding each other and crying. I rolled down the window on my side. "Who are they?" I wondered out loud. "I don't recognize any of them," Dennis answered. "Why won't they leave? Why are they staying? That should be us down there." "No," my husband answered, "we'd better leave now, if only for the children," and he pointed off to the side. There stood a yellow-orange bulldozer, waiting its turn. One man

reached in and started the motor as if to hurry the girls along;
another leaned against it smoking a cigarette. The girls continued to cry and hold each other as Dennis turned our van
toward home.

FOUR

Grief

My God, my God, why have you abandoned me?
—Psalm 22:1

Morning came again. To my amazement, the birds still sang, the wind still whistled, the darkness of night folded, and once again the earth was clothed in dawn. "Oh, no, another day," I thought. This became my waking thought for many more days to come. As I lay in bed listening to the twittering of the birds calling to each other and welcoming the sunrise, I resented their joyful exuberance. Surely they must know the shadow of death is our visitor. Why would they not be silent—why would the sun shine? Each morning angered me anew. It was so hard to make my body get out of bed. I was never a morning person, but now I was completely unwilling to face the day. It seemed I had hardly slept, as I continued each night to awaken almost every hour.

Last night, I was sure that I had heard Lisa crying softly in her bed, and she called out my name. What cruel tricks my imagination played on me! I walked slowly to her room, knowing she would not be there, turned on the overhead light and sat down on the top step. Three-fifteen, her alarm clock smiled at me from across the room. Pretty room—clean, cozy, empty, lifeless. "Why, oh why?" I cried and I screamed out to the room. "It's not fair!" I cried myself to sleep lying on the purple carpeting. Then I awakened again, in a state of semi-confusion, at four-thirty-five. I wandered around the other bedrooms, checking on the other children to see if they were still breathing. Finally, I collapsed in my own bed, a feeling of heaviness deep within, and dozed fitfully for a few more hours. Now the day had truly begun, and with great effort I got out of bed and slowly walked over to the purple room and peeked in. It was still empty.

Breakfast did not seem at all appealing to me, as I placed the cereal bowls on the kitchen table and reached for the baby's bottle. "Lisa will not be eating with us this morning," I thought. "Lisa will not ever be eating again." Death was so final. It came and took everything, period. She would never again stand in this kitchen, I thought, never again laugh or cry—we'll never hear her voice again! I dissolved in tears, sobbing loudly. "Oh God, no, no! Somebody, anybody, help me get through this day." No one sat in her place at the table.

I decided to eat a doughnut while I fed the baby her bottle. There was so much food in the house. The refrigerator was filled to capacity with all shapes and sizes of dishes puzzled in together; countertops also held various aluminum-covered and plastic-wrapped edibles. People had been so generous and I had not been in a mood to cook. Whatever happened to be around is what we ate. It didn't seem to matter to me what we ate or *if* we ate, or at what time of day. Although I was a firm believer in proper nutrition, even to the point of health foods and organic gardening, it didn't matter to me right now. We had ample supplies of food and the next meal became whatever couldn't fit into the fridge or whatever anybody wanted at the moment. I had skipped meals yesterday, or actually I had forgotten to eat. I never seemed to be hungry anymore, although some days eating became an easy way to pass the time of day. How I welcomed distractions these days. The television became the most excellent diversion. That noisy square box sang and danced and bathed the room in color and frivolity tugging at my mind and turning it in different directions. Like a master deceiver it pulled my thoughts away from the reality of the moment to whatever was behind curtain number three. And I let it lead me to foolish areas of no importance. Reality was too painful.

My mind toyed with the idea of getting drunk this morning. What a strange thought—how foreign to my mind. I had not had liquor in ten?—twenty years? We didn't even keep anything in the house stronger than "decaf." But it was only a short drive to the carry-out. Quick and easy consolation, I reasoned, and it would bring some measure of relief from my distress, only temporary albeit. . . . My mind struggled to reject these thoughts that somehow were so inviting—wasn't temporary relief better than no relief? Where are you God when I need you! And now, the phone began its monotonous occupation of calling to me all day. I consistently ignored this disturbance in anger at its ill-timed demands on my attention.

I gathered my children into the van to "take a little ride and get out of the house." After starting the motor, we moved down the hill; the baby already began to be lulled to sleep by the motion. "Where are we going, mommy?" the others chattered. "Oh, just for a ride," I answered absent-mindedly. "Where *are* we going?" I considered this question—the mall . . . the supermarket . . . the library . . . the carry-out? "O Lord, help me!" I cried. "Where can I go?" I could think of no place to go, no safe shelter, no one who would accept me as this disordered being incapable of functioning on a rational level, no friendship so secure as to stand the test of unconditional acceptance of my wretched condition.

The van found its way to the cemetery as it had every morning since the funeral; up a little hill, around a curve, one more curve and there it was. A cold, hard stone standing in silent testimony of life snatched away in the blossoming of youth. I got out of the van and walked slowly to the grave. The green carpeting of spring grass was interrupted by the 4 x 8 foot plot of fresh sunken dirt which seemed to be cruelly boasting of its latest arrival. I fell to my knees in the muddy rectangle, sobbing uncontrollably, barely aware of my children behind me in the van. "What is left?" I thought. "Is this all that is left after seventeen years?" Time stood still . . . and passed very quickly. My emotions somehow gave in to reason, and we left the graveyard.

It was still early morning, and the day lay gaping its jaws waiting to devour me. Was I losing my mind? At times, I believed I surely was. I walked through each day struggling to keep my balance on the edge of an enormous chasm of unthinkable depth. The experience compelled me to walk on the edge, always. It was hard work to say the least, requiring great strength and energy. I fought vigorously, striving to maintain my equilibrium suspended in the air between two opposing forces. "The edge," as I called it, seemed to be formed into a continuous circle. Like a tightrope-walker, I walked around and around in constant danger of losing my footing. All the signs cautioned me, "Bear to the right," and I tried to lean that way against a raging windstorm buffeting my body. If I could only force myself to the right before I lost control completely. In that direction was everything I believed in and could hang onto. But I was powerless to take command of the situation; and the harsh storm continued to wash away familiar landmarks and footholds.

As I stayed on my perilous course, the area to the left was marked "Caution—Dead End" and "No Outlet." I couldn't see anything on that side because it was too deep and dark; but I sensed danger and knew if I fell that way, all would be truly and finally lost. I braced myself against the increasing violence of the storm, any minute expecting to fall off the edge. With both arms extended I barely maintained a shaky balance amidst the ensuing conflict, trying to hang on by the skin of my teeth until the storm passed.

"Let's sort out this clothing," said my husband, "and give it to someone." We were in the purple room again. We seemed to be drawn there so much, perhaps because vestiges of Lisa remained there, signs and traces of her life with us. "We'll make three piles," he continued, so methodical and business-like, "one over here for her girlfriends; one here for things that fit you and you want to keep; and another over there to give to the used clothing store." And with the closets open, we began. All the decisions, however, seemed to fall to me. Did this fit me? Did I want it? Would I wear it? What about Anne . . . Sarah . . . the needy? Some things I couldn't decide and I threw them in a plastic trash bag. Every article of clothing brought me to a different time, a different place—school outfits, church outfits, prom gowns, show choir clothing, jeans and sweaters galore, and enough shoes to fit a parade of size-six feet. There was her band uniform to go to the cleaners, outfits borrowed and traded to be returned to other girls, clothing that belonged to me, a jacket that belonged to a boyfriend, her father's shirts, my mauve blouse that I had searched all over for last year, her confirmation and first communion dresses, and an angel costume that I had made ten years ago complete with wings and halo. Fresh grief washed over me again and again. Part of me wanted to leave everything in her closet forever, part of me wanted to throw everything away in anger, and part of me wanted someone else to make all these decisions. I struggled not to fall off the edge.

Another day I cleaned out her small lavender desk nestled in the corner by the french doors. As I sorted through the typical teenage stuff, I fought the impulse to empty the contents of the four drawers into a trash bag. This would avoid the pain of sorting through everything, and I could put the bag neatly in the attic and not think about it. "What should I do with all of this?" . . . a diary, a pocket Bible, a pocket calculator, pens, pencils, school papers, writing paper, a dictionary. Then I spied it—there in the top drawer, an envelope sealed and marked "Mom" with her very own handwriting. Opening it I read:

Mommy—

I'm writing this so you will at least have a penmanship sample after I'm gone.

Smile mommy—please be strong. This is by far the hardest letter to write. I feel like the perfect team is being split up. You were always the right, I was the left. But—I beat you here! And is it great!

I know our relationship worked mostly because of you. I'm a stubborn pain—I'm sorry. However there were so many times when our minds "locked," and we were thinking exactly alike. I'll never forget the piano lamp or the kitty puzzle.

What I want to say here is you were *always* my best friend. No one else loved, cared, or shared like you. I love you as a mother, as a confidante, as a friend.

Thank you for loving me.

> "Let us build the city of God,
> may your tears be turned into dancing.
> For the Lord our light and our love
> has turned the night into day."

Lisa
XOXO

"L - i - s - a . . . L - i - s - a." I cried out loud in pain and anguish: "Don't go . . . please come back . . . don't leave me, I love you . . . please, please, come back . . . God . . . help me . . . help me now. . . ."

I did not want to write the thank you notes, even though Dennis kept insisting. I was truly grateful for all that people had done for us, but to write it out in hundreds of little notes was definitely above and beyond the call of duty in my weakened state. I sat in my favorite brown chair trying with my depleted reserves to decide to write those notes. Everything in my life seemed to be an insurmountable task, a crisis calling for a major act of the will. How difficult it was to handle even small issues. Dennis wrote the notes with the help of my girlfriend. I watched the two of them sitting at the table. He handled these things so much better than I. What I knew in my mind and my heart to be the right thing to do, I seemed powerless to carry out in reality. I was unable to meet the demands of life and the expectations of society, of people in general.

I continued to go over all the events of Lisa's death in my mind, like a motion picture screen painfully rolling the images of the past events over and over again. My apathy to the present situation was only surpassed by this constant repetition of the past. Life had dealt me such a fatal blow. I was helpless to live in the present and hopeless about the future. How long would this continue? When could I begin to care again? How do you mend a broken heart?

Days turned into weeks, and weeks turned into months. It seemed as though my child had been dead for a million years; and then again, it seemed like only yesterday. I abandoned all of my regular routine and my life turned into a test of survival, as I treaded water fiercely to keep from drowning. The battle raged on inside of me and my thought process became unclear and disturbed. I began to experience the feeling of being in a deep pit, with darkness shrouding me, cold and damp. Had I fallen off the edge? I feared that I must have!

An oppressive force crushed my heart, cruel and heavy on my chest, making breathing a difficult task. Maybe I was having a heart attack—oh blessed relief! no more struggling! And then, more waves of grief came crushing over me, overpowering as a tyrant holding me down in the bottom of a murky pit. Nothing made sense anymore as I was driven to the brink of despair again and again by an unseen enemy. I was physically, emotionally, and spiritually exhausted and could offer little resistance to such an opposing force. Oh from where would my help come?

Grief was a one-on-one match, a solitary struggle. Such a great force is not opposable and I feared I was losing the battle. Lacking the ability to pray or even cry, I remained powerless to climb out of the pit. No light shone on my mind. No strength surged up from within. No peace surpassed all understanding. My life had turned to ashes, there was no longer meaning in anything. Nothing is true, everything is a lie. Grief weighed heavily upon my mind and spirit, ruling with a heavy hand, treating me harshly and unjustly. Eventually, I was no longer frightened, as I slipped in and out of this bottomless pit of tyranny. I was simply worn out. I had nothing to hang onto, nothing was left . . . no comfort . . . no relief in sight.

FIVE

God

Lord, to whom would we go? You have the words that
give eternal life.

—John 6:68

My first experience with God happened in my adolescent
years. What a tumultuous time of life, confusing for me and
difficult. Through the bewilderment of change and growth,
God touched my life with an awareness of his presence. It is
a vivid memory imprinted forever on my mind. It was summer time. Wearing a green plaid skirt and a white blouse, I
was sitting on the edge of my bed in my bedroom. I can
picture the white furniture, the wicker chair in the corner
cluttered with clothing, and the small white table and stool
in front of the window. In utter discouragement bordering
on despair, I cried out to God. It was not a glorious moment
filled with feelings of rapture, nor did the circumstances in
my life change; but I was left with three certainties: God was
real, God cared about me, and I would see God face-to-face

one day. My life did not dramatically change, nor did I; but I carried my secret within me, and I thought about it often.

As my life continued to unfold, I "tuned in" to God at certain times here and there along the way. Sometimes I prayed with great intensity and purpose; and at other times I all but forgot God completely—barely remembering the secret he had entrusted to me so many years ago. With the birth of our first child, came a period of much joy and happiness in my life. I named her Lisa because that name meant "consecrated to God." What a lovely tiny bundle of innocence and life. I knew that God had loaned her to me, and I thanked him with heartfelt joy. And then I went about the busyness of my life, with alternating periods of knowing and loving God—and other times of being unmoved by his grandeur, unaware of his caring for me, and insensitive to his presence.

Shortly after the birth of our second child, I had a life-changing experience. I now took God seriously and the secret came alive within me. I still lived my ordinary life with its daily routines; but now God became a part of everything. I possessed a heightened awareness of the reality of God pervading every aspect of my life. Menial tasks took on new meaning; I was headed back to God. The busyness of life became filled with purpose. I belonged to him—he belonged to me. We would work our way through life together. How simple it all seemed. How thankful I was. Life held meaning.

"A woman of the Lord," they called me. "She would work her way through this death and grief." "She's known God for years." I had felt God preparing me from the moment we knew of Lisa's cancer. Prayer and scripture had been a part of my life for so many years, learning to trust in God, growing to have faith in his promises. I felt certain he would see me through. Driving along the busy interstate on my way to the hospital, I prayed and sang psalms. We would find out today how advanced the cancer was. The meeting was still an hour away, so I would have time to visit with Lisa before the doctors arrived. I was anxious to see her. I had missed her since she had been in the hospital, and seeing her once a day wasn't enough. I also felt a sense of peace deep within and I wanted to be near her hoping she would sense my calmness and be comforted.

Glancing in the rearview mirror, I noticed two red trucks moving to pass me in the left-hand lane . . . Lisa had had her spleen removed and wouldn't be coming home today. The first red truck passed my car and written on the side was the word "ADVANCED." She would be disappointed at not being able to come home; but we would chat and joke, and watch TV, and read magazines, and being together would make both of us feel better. The second red truck passed my car and written on the side was "Aurora Casket Company." I stopped singing and I stopped praying and I thought about those two red trucks the rest of the drive.

Lisa was in a great deal of pain when I arrived. We did not laugh and talk or watch TV. I prayed with her, wanting her pain to go away, but it didn't. The girl in the other bed was perky and cheerful. She had some type of muscular problem. She told us to "trust in the Lord" and he would see us through. Of course this was true, but her words echoed with emptiness. The doctor told us Lisa's cancer was in the advanced stages. She cried. We would sign papers for chemotherapy next week. Her chances were excellent they said.

My faith remained strong and my life of prayer grew and deepened. I didn't know for sure if Lisa would live or die, but I believed that it was in God's hands. I felt God guiding me and speaking to me in scripture and strengthening me through people. Books on death came to me through the mail and I devoured them. I knew that we were headed for difficult times, but I firmly believed that God would hold my hand and bring me through. He would be present to me as this frightening storm raged and he would speak the words, "Be still and know that I am Lord." That would be enough to calm the turbulent seas and we would walk through it together. But when Lisa died . . . God died too.

With death came a cloud of darkness that obscured

everything my faith stood on. The curtain descended and all meaning became dim and unclear. God was silent, and it seemed as if he had completely removed himself from the situation. He was unable to communicate through this dense shroud of death. He could not or would not break through. "But God," I cried out, "you called me beloved. You gave me your Presence. You put your hand on my life! Where are you when I need you the most?"

Silence and silence.

"Footprints in the sand," my mind thought. "When there was only one set of footprints, it was then that I carried you."

"No good! I can't see it, feel it, sense it, know it! It doesn't feel like you are carrying me. It seems as though you have thrown me down, dropped me like a hot potato, discarded me as useless!"

Silence and silence and silence.

"Can this be true?" I thought, "Was it all a lie? Was I deceived? Did I really have a spiritual life? God, are you really real? Help me!"

Silence and silence.

"O God, you are my God. Hasten to help me. My heart is nearly broken with sorrow. I am overcome with pain. O Lord, it hurts so badly. Come to my assistance, I beg you."

Silence and silence.

"O Lord, you told me you loved me but I forgot. Please tell me again."

Silence.

No comfort or relief rescued me from the valley of the shadow of death, as I became overwhelmed with doubts and uncertainties. Meaningless thoughts and feelings of despair assailed me at all times and I feared I would not survive.

Eventually, I stopped struggling. I gave up trying to pray, and trying to know God's will, and trying to understand. The battle was over and I didn't even know if I had won or lost. The darkness seemed to lift a little and I sorted out my thoughts. God is still real whether I can feel him or not. My child is still dead whether I can understand or not. I must go on with life whether I want to or not. "Everything is a decision," I thought. And a small prayer formed within my secret place . . . "You said you would *always* love me. You said you would *never* leave me. You promised."

And life continued, and grief waged its bitter onslaught, and I let it. The pain was still deadening and it was difficult to live through each day. I clung to his promise. God was real. He said he would always love me. He said he would never leave me. He promised. I seemed void of feeling. I couldn't convince myself that this was true; but I decided to believe it. I thought of my wedding vows . . . I take you forever, in good times and bad times, for richer or poorer, in sickness and in health.

Spring came again the next year. We had planted a hundred purple crocus bulbs all over Lisa's grave. Driving through the cemetery, I was anxious to check on their arrival. Had they blossomed? The grass was still brown, and a light frost covered everything. It was a crisp, cool morning as I drove the familiar route—up a little hill, around a curve, one more curve and there it was. We could see it even in the distance, a blanket of deep purple covering the grave, defying the frost and yellow grass, blossoming boldly through the bleakness of the graveyard, a herald of spring. I knew that winter would give way to spring; but somehow, now I could also see that spring would once again blossom in my heart.

Those tiny purple buds peeked out at me through the frost proclaiming openly their new life. And I began to see that the promises I clung to so fiercely for myself, were also true for my child. My life looked like that graveyard. Death had encamped there, and it was spread throughout, cold, empty and desolate. But right here in this tiny little patch, a seed had been planted. And without me realizing how it was nurtured, it began to grow unbeknown to me. And now it sprang forth, not in full bloom yet, but a small bud just beginning to blossom with its promise of fullness.

The secret was still true. God is real, and he does care for me, and I will see him face-to-face, one day.

SIX

Memories

Blessed are they who mourn for they will be comforted.
—Matthew 5:4

It's a girl! My first born. What a joyous moment for a mother! After months of waiting, and caring, and carrying, and anticipating, through hours of pain and struggling, new life emerges . . . a blossom of innocence, a promise of love, hope for the future.

What a wonderful childhood Lisa enjoyed. An only child for ten years, we doted on her, and coddled her. She could do no wrong. Every smile or laugh was precious and refreshing; every outburst was tolerated as self-expression. Each milestone in life was celebrated as a momentous occasion. Her first word, first step, first tooth all were notable achievements which we magnified and applauded. Never once did a thought of the intruder, Death, enter my mind. We had no experience with this Grim Reaper, not so much as a passing acquaintance. No one close to us had yet been introduced to this thief of life. We were a young couple with a wonderful only child. Life was good; and we fully enjoyed it.

Lisa grew and matured amidst all the ordinary, everyday experiences of life. And my love for her grew and changed in many different ways as she grew and changed in many different ways. Lisa was always a demanding child—outspoken and extremely bright. I remember her first steps at ten months old. They were so bold and definite, no ballerina tiptoes, but a trailblazer in workboots for sure. She had a seriousness about her that was evident at a very early age. "Serious baby," I penned in her baby album; she wore a look of pondering the problems of the world. At two years old, a department store photographer refused to take her picture because he could not get her to smile. "She always looks like this," I urged. "Go on and take it. This is her usual look." People told us, as early as two or three, that she acted much older than her years.

Then in kindergarten her teacher wrote on her report card: "Lisa thinks that she is the teacher and she often instructs the children in what they should and should not do!"

Her first communion day stands out as one of my best memories. Her innocence and openness shone through the seriousness of her nature and imprinted a smile on my mothering heart. She was a picture of truth that day. Her face reflected the awe of the Almighty, and yet, in a child-like way, she was eager and unafraid. Later during the afternoon at her party, she gave several of her presents to her best friend, in such a kind and generous manner that my mind recalled his words, "Unless you become as little children you shall not enter the kingdom of God." By second grade, we had been thoroughly informed that we had a gifted child, well-above-average intelligence with an insatiable quest for the path unknown, someone with a pioneer spirit, a leader in new ventures.

As Lisa grew into adolescence, we met with many conflicts as we struggled to shape this adventuresome spirit to fit in an ordinary, average slot suited to our expectations of what a teen should be. She was so creative and dramatic. I continually made a strong effort to shape her into a more quiet, docile character, the proverbial folly of trying to fit a square peg into a round hole. Why did I do this? Why couldn't I allow her to be who she was? Does this mean that I didn't accept her for herself? Did I in essence reject who she was? Did I not fully love her? Why did I try to change her instead of guiding or directing her? I have no answers. O God! You gave me the most difficult job in the world—and I couldn't take a course on how to do it!

Lisa loved to stand out in a crowd, to be different, to be noticed. I, on the other hand, am the hidden, blending, unnoticed personality type. Was I unconsciously trying to make her like me? What an influence I exerted upon this unfolding personality to conform to my specifications. Now, my hindsight so much sharper than my insight, it seems like the natural order of events for conflict to ensue. Lisa's personality was self-assured and she was not easily intimidated. She was also stubborn and strong-willed, and so am I. We should have noticed the storm clouds gathering. Maybe then we could have prepared for the turbulence of metamorphosis, growth, change. Instead, I valiantly fought to contain this whirlwind of developing childhood into my carton that was neatly labeled, "Quiet, studious, hard-working, sensible, predictable." Lisa was nothing like that. Lisa was not mature—and neither was I.

Not all of my memories are happy ones. Life has held hard times and hard memories. We had our share of disagreements, family feuds, and arguments. I said and did things poorly. I said and did things wonderfully. I wish our relationship was perfect. It was not perfect; life is not perfect. Our relationship was blemished by all the imperfections that daily life in a family holds. And I grieve for Lisa's childhood and all the mistakes I made with my first job of mothering. I wish that I could go back and do things differently. My mothering heart, furrowed with the pains of grief, cries out in anger: "It's not fair!" "If only I had known!" "It's not my fault!"

And yet, whose fault could it be? That sneaky, sly attacker, that thief in the night, that robber—Death! You have taken my first born, deprived me of a mother's natural rights, stolen my hope for the future. But the doorway to the grave is silent, and not clearly visible to my human eyes, and deaf to my cries for justice. And so the pain of grief continues to carve ruts into my already broken heart.

A vivid picture in my memory of events is prom night. Now, this Cinderella event each year becomes an excavation project in the inner recesses of my memories, hollowing out and uncovering the ruins of reminiscence. How I wish this yearly occurrence could be discontinued and the words "prom night" never be spoken or heard again. We took the Volkswagen shopping so Lisa could do the driving. She had eagerly adopted this inexpensive second vehicle as "her wheels." It was a brisk but sunny February Saturday, as we headed through town, just the two of us, gown shopping. Lisa was positively overflowing with gleeful anticipation of an exciting day at the mall trying on dozens of dresses, flowing with yards of taffeta and satin. I was, naturally, much less excited, but still very content with the day, welcoming the opportunity to be with her when she was in such a happy mood. These past months of chemotherapy were such an exhausting, trying time for our whole family. It now seemed good to be headed to the mall on this interstate instead of to the medical center.

Lisa decided to take the next exit and try a local bridal shop before going to the mall. It was there that we found the "perfect dress." "Oh, Lisa, I don't know. It's not at all what I had in mind," I began. "Oh, it's absolutely perfect!" she insisted. "Don't you just love the color!" It was dark forest green taffeta with shimmering black highlights. "Well, dear, it *is* a very regal looking color, and it *does* look good on you," I said, "but I was thinking more pastel, you know, pink or powder blue . . . something spring looking." "Oh, mom, everybody will be wearing pastel; this is so different, so individual, so dramatic." The sales clerk was on her side; and it was, after all, *on sale*, too! "Great," I said as we left the small shop with our elegant dark green formal in a hanging bag, "Now we don't have to shop the whole day. We can go home and get some work done." "Oh please," begged Lisa, "let's go to the mall anyway! We can shop for earrings and a necklace, don't forget shoes; and I can try on lots of other gowns just to make sure we bought the right one!" Since I had already decided that this was her day to spend as she liked, off to the mall we went.

Now, as she descended the long staircase in our living room her attitude seemed to defy the cancer that attempted to take hold of her life. Of course she looked beautiful, but my eye was focused on deeper issues. Behind the surface of beauty in dark green taffeta, still lurked the Intruder. Her stylish coiffured hair-do was in reality a wig covering a peach-fuzz scalp—vestiges of toxic chemicals that had become members of the family. The glittering beaded choker around her neck skillfully covered scars from surgery to remove lymph nodes. The elbow length gloves hid needle tracks and bruises from needles. Life and death, in a tug-of-war, wrapped up in green taffeta . . . off to the prom. How do you mend a broken heart?

And then it was Christmas. This would be our last Christmas with Lisa, and we all knew it. I, for one, refused to enter into the festivities of the season. I had already mentally cancelled the event, crossed it off my calendar. "Mommy, mommy, can we put the Christmas stencils on the window panes?" my younger children chorused. "No, not now," I answered. "Maybe later," I lied. "Golly, I just love these stencils!" Lisa announced to the children. "*We'll* do them instead of mom this year. You get the spray snow. You get the trash bag. I'll get the scissors. 'Joy to the World'" she hummed quietly. Bah humbug, I felt. How could we possibly get through Christmas this year? Indeed, this was too heavy a burden, too much to ask from mere mortal beings. But the rest of the world did not seem to realize the tremendous crisis at hand.

As the holiday season continued its approach, costumed Santas ho-ho-ho'd in the department stores and on street corners. Decorations adorned downtown streets and private homes. Even on our own street, brightly colored lights twinkled, and the world in general seemed to come alive with the hustle-bustle of festive preparations. I couldn't escape it; it was everywhere. Why, this season seemed so shallow and materialistic! I cried easily, daily. Was life truly so superficial? I tried to meditate on the real meaning of Christmas, the birth of Christ—"This day in Bethlehem a child is born, he is Christ the Lord . . ." This brought on even more tears. Nothing made sense. Lisa decorated the whole house that year. She seemed so peaceful and calm, while I struggled to keep my sanity.

Lisa shopped very carefully that year and selected a present for each family member that seemed to say, "You'll have this to remember me by when I'm gone." And I frantically bought her everything she ever wanted, as though the presents could speak for me my silent thoughts—"Don't leave me, I love you."

And now, on the other side of death, what is left? My mind frequently saunters through the corridors of memory, peeking in every door. I feel compelled to open each and every door. Some doors are closed tightly and open only with much difficulty. Other doors I open again and again. What's left? We have given away all of her things, and changed her room completely into a different room. We no longer say "Lisa's room." There is no longer "Lisa's place" at the table or "Lisa's seat" in the car. Her class has graduated from high school—and some from college. Her boyfriend has since gotten married. What's left?

The first year after her death, we received three phone calls. "Is Lisa there?" the caller asked. It took my breath away, so surprised was I. "No, I'm sorry she's not here," I replied truthfully. Two were from girls she had met at camp in another city, one from a young man away in the service. We also received a few letters addressed to her. Two were from out of town girls. One was a college acceptance letter. Lots of graduation literature and junk mail came that year. I hoped each day that she would get mail so I could read her name on the envelope. After a while nothing more came.

What's left? I still have the 1 oz. perfume bottle she gave me that last Christmas. I tried not to use the perfume too much so I could save it forever; but it evaporated. I have the slippers and night dress she bought for me—both threadbare from wearing them almost every night for two years.

What's left? Lisa loved to write and she kept a journal since sixth grade. I have four large, spiral notebooks filled with her own thoughts in her own handwriting. Toward the end she wrote prayers and cries to God. I have a dozen poems she wrote. I have a letter she wrote to the Holy Spirit just before her confirmation day. And I have numerous letters and notes and cards that she sent to me, her mother.

What's left? A stone in the cemetery with her name on it. But she's not under that stone. She is free and unencumbered. And I am restrained, banished, in mourning and weeping in this valley of tears.

What's left? Only the memories in my heart, and the belief that I will see her again someday.

What's left? . . .

SEVEN

Life

I know that I will live to see
the Lord's goodness in this present life.
Trust in the Lord.
Have faith, do not despair.
Trust in the Lord.

—Psalm 27:13-14

It was a very large helium balloon, probably two feet in diameter, one of those metallic foil-looking kind. It was plain silver on one side. The other side was pink, with a picture of a stork holding a bundle. Printed on it were the words, "It's a girl." As I ascended our living room staircase holding this balloon, I knew that something was different inside of me. This was the very staircase that Lisa had descended in her green taffeta gown. This was the very staircase that Lisa had hoped to descend in a flowing white wedding gown. This was the very staircase that my husband had descended carrying Lisa's lifeless body.

And now, I walked up each step slowly and deliberately. "What is this stirring, this feeling inside of me?" I wondered. "Something is new and different." I tried to put a label on it. Excitement? No, not excitement—too big. Happy? No, definitely not happy. Alive? No, not quite that animated. Aware? That's it! There was a new awareness inside of me, a new realization of an old truth. Lisa had gone to God. "Well, of course," I chided myself, "you knew that all along." That's why I had brought the helium balloon to the cemetery the day we buried her. I could still picture it hurrying to the clouds as we stood around her casket.

But somehow, this was different. I had reached the top of the stairs. The purple room beckoned me at the end of the hallway. Slowly I moved toward our lavender sanctuary, the helium balloon dancing above my head. I threw open the veranda doors and sunlight spilled onto the purple carpeting as I stepped out on the balcony. What I knew in my head had somehow been awakened in my heart. She's alive in a new way! She's alive in a new life! The secret is true! God is real, and he cares for Lisa, and they have met each other face-to-face!

I released the helium balloon and it hastened heavenward, frolicking and twirling as it glistened in the sunshine. I stood motionless watching. "It's a girl," I whispered to God, "but of course, you know that." Just then, grief crashed into my private revelation and hot tears streamed down my cheeks in silent protest. I watched the balloon get smaller and smaller—it was barely the size of a pinhead. The sun reflected one last time off the metallic foil sending me a wink of a sparkle and then it was gone. Or at least, because I could no longer see it, it seemed gone to me. But I could still picture it high above the clouds, glimmering and dancing in the sunshine.

Dying is easy, I thought as I came back down to earth and to the living room . . . living is hard. "Oh, Lisa, you took the easy way out," I reprimanded her one last time, "and you left me here with the harder part." But love does not die. The script of her life is written in my heart and it still glistens in the corridors of my memory. But at the same time, the spotlight radiates its beam upon a new life—in the realm of mystery, something unseen and unknown—enlightening my innermost vision. It is a hint, a whisper, an inkling; grief is still a sledge hammer, a bulldozer, a trench digger. Yet the taste of new life remains, with its gentle touch, tracing seedlings of awareness into my hurt-furrowed heart. "Oh Lord, I do believe," I prayed. "Please help the part of me that doesn't believe."

"What's in the box?" I asked my girlfriend. "This is a present that was sent to me by an old friend," she answered, "but I think it belongs to you." I watched her open the slim, white box and, discarding the tissue paper, she revealed a mobile of hot-air balloons of different sizes and colors connected by thread. As she lifted the main thread higher into the air, the balloons layered into a colorful cascade, twirling and spinning, each connected by a single thread which brought life to all.

We fastened it to the crystal chandelier above the dining room table. It was entrancing and beautiful to watch. Bathed in the softly tinted hues of the crystal, it performed its rhythmic unpatterned movements to a silent melody. How fragile it seemed, hanging there by a thread. Yet, it was flowing freely, so capable of changing and moving from one place to another. "I want to be that mobile, Lord," I prayed. "Make me capable of responding easily and quickly to your slightest whisperings in my heart."

Spring came again this year and I cautiously welcomed its arrival. My heart, shocked by death, scarred with grief, and kneaded by pain into a new softness, seemed to have acquired sight. Not unlike insight, and not unlike hindsight, it possessed an awakening heart-sight, a new way of looking at the world, a sense of heightened awareness once again. Every facet of springtime seemed to rouse this inner vision, kindling a spark of faith in life renewed. The bare branches of trees, seemingly dry sticks, once again budded into greenery painting the horizons. Bulbs and seeds, that were shriveled and brown, blossomed in beauty splashing color over all. The carpet of brown covering the earth was once again transposed into greenness. The green spoke to me in wonder of its amazement, marveling at the transformation that had occurred. Signs of life-changes surrounded me, and boldly proclaimed their silent witness of faith in a master artist.

The mourning doves had nested this year in many locations on our property. The children had been eagerly awaiting the arrival of baby birds and had even named the nesting ladies. One tolerant mother, named Millie, had the courage to build her nest on the basketball hoop, steadying it against the backboard. All ball games had been understandably cancelled until Millie's babies hatched. The children waited patiently checking daily with upturned faces unable to determine any progress. Millie stayed put, her plump brownish body fluffed out over the nest. But this day, as I pulled my car into the driveway, the nest was empty. There on the steps to our deck, was a dead baby bird. I looked up at the basketball hoop which still held on to the empty nest, and then back down at the dead bird. I cried as I buried Millie's baby. Her distant mournful coo-coo-coo was audible. I knew I wanted that nest taken down, because it was no longer needed.

Climbing bittersweet covered the thickets and woods, but, living in town I couldn't find a trace of it. It wasn't that I admired this woody vine with its small green flowers, nor was I even attracted to its distinctive bi-colored fruit. I simply was enamored of its name. Bittersweet. What a word on my tongue that tasted of my life. Bittersweet, a taste of death and a taste of God, together like salt and pepper, bread and butter. Where was that vine? Bittersweet—surely it was blossoming somewhere besides being wound around my heart. Bittersweet—distasteful but savory, painful yet perfumed, acrid and fragrant, brutal but balmy—death and God, causing discomfort and hardship but so full of hope and promise. Bittersweet—life at its best . . . or worst—life to the full.

My heart-sight still catches glimpses of Lisa's new life in that metallic balloon, shimmering and dancing in the sun far above the clouds. I can picture her running on a straight path, holding up the billowy skirts of the taffeta prom gown that we buried her in. She is smiling a radiant beaming smile and looking straight ahead as she races to life on high. God is running from the other side of the path, with outstretched arms coming to meet her in an embrace of love. Sometimes I picture her, still in her burial gown, at a heavenly prom dancing with saints of old. And then, I can see her in a white garment, walking hand in hand with Jesus. They are looking at each other; and they are smiling. Then they both smile at me.

My life is in the mobile, hanging by a thread, suspended in mid-air. I peek into the dining room, dark and empty, and there it hangs, motionless and silent. There is not even the slightest movement now; where before it turned around freely and moved in many directions. It has quieted itself in the darkness, each member of every section stilled, all segments dangling separately yet together in suspended animation, calmed and hushed. However, it is still held together by the Master thread as it waits in readiness to yield to the slightest touch . . . to be swayed by the softest whispering . . . to be enlivened by the gentlest breeze. . . .

Breathe on me, breath of God.

EIGHT

Pieces

The world will make you suffer. But be brave!
I have defeated the world.

—John 16:33

"They" told me that time heals. Give it time. It will get better in time. Perhaps I should say Time. They said Time heals all wounds. But it does not seem to hold that power for me. It has been some time now since Lisa died, and my life still seems difficult to manage with ease. The tears are right there waiting to spill over at any moment.

I feel fragmented, broken in pieces like a puzzle all spread out on the table. None of the pieces are together and I am not even sure if they fit together. There are so many pieces that I fear I will not be able to put them back together. Is it an insurmountable task? Some of the pieces look easier to work with than others. These are more brightly colored and have pictures of faces on them. There are many of these pieces—

children's faces, adult faces, familiar faces, and some that I don't recognize. But these pieces are scattered and interspersed with all the others . . . I can identify my children's faces and my husband's. There are also relatives, friends who want to help, friends who want to avoid me, neighbors, work relationships, church relationships. All of the pieces are staring up at me as if wondering where they fit in place . . . a formidable task of sorting.

Other parts of the puzzle are strewn haphazardly about. They are more darkly colored in a vastly different array of hues, standing out boldly in clusters of colors that readily attract my eyes. They represent my life in terms of what I do—my work in the home. These pieces are scattered all throughout the picture touching various other parts of the puzzle. There are an enormous number of them staring up at me, demanding my attention at every glance. I want to avoid looking at them, perhaps because they are so numerous.

Another segment of this group is clumped in corners. Farther removed and harder to reach, they represent my work in writing and music, creative talents once alive, now dormant, showing no signs of activity. I feel a small stirring of desire to reach these pieces but they are too removed and I am unable to stretch the distance. I look at them remembering past consolation, but incapable still of the extension. My gaze settles somewhat comfortably on these pieces, however it is quickly captured, even seized against its will, to recognize a very dark and strangely shaped grouping.

These pieces are unpleasant to the eye and I am immediately uninterested in working with them. Nevertheless, my focus remains captured for the time being, and I cautiously examine the structure of these less desirable pieces. They are all black, with sharp edges and jagged borders. They represent the pain in my life. I quickly avert my eyes once again but I am just as quickly recaptured against my will. I have acknowledged their presence. They compel me to look at them. The visual examination detects shades of blackness, strange and murky texturing. The lighter areas are somewhat less painful to look at but still speckled with sharp edges . . . the pain of others not understanding, the pain of people thinking I am over it by now, the pain of others forgetting entirely. The pieces quickly darken, as water darkens a blackboard, washing into the pain of powerlessness. I am unable to do anything about the situation.

The rest of these pieces are coal black with innumerable jagged edges. I don't understand how they can possibly fit into the puzzle. Their shape is too awful to unite with the rest of the puzzle pieces. They are the pain of death, of my child's death, of my daughter's death, of Lisa's death. They represent death itself and all the finality that comes with it. As I survey the entire puzzle spread out on the table of my life, I notice these coal black jagged pieces are everywhere and they touch every other piece. Many of the brightly colored pieces are partially or entirely covered by these darkened misfits. Why would it be impossible for me to put this puzzle together with so many of these distorted configurations?

All of a sudden it seems so clear how to begin this puzzle. I need to get all of these strange pieces out of the way. Maybe then I can work with what is left. And so I begin to pick up the ugly pieces, the very pieces I am so uninterested in working with, and I put them in my hand. I continue to gather these distasteful fragments but the coal black pieces are too many for my hand and I improvise with my arm against my body; this forces me to hold the pieces closer to me, in essence to hug them to myself. Nevertheless, I continue to pick them up. After all, they *do* belong to my puzzle although I cannot figure out where; and they *are* part of the whole picture though I don't know how. I pick them all up, cradling them in my arm, holding them closely, jagged edges and all. They are *my* pieces; they are my pain. I own them; I claim them. I will somehow figure out how to put the puzzle together, even though I have to work with these dark jagged pieces.

Off to the side is yet another bunch of pieces, quite ordinary looking in color and shape but they appear to be worn, maybe even faded. Some of them are folded or creased; others have been ripped and torn. These pieces seem to be very easy to work with. Many of them are straight border edges and others are simple shapes that could be easily interlocked. These pieces represent my health: nutrition, exercise, sleep and rest, attitude. I have a tendency to begin on this side of the puzzle. I think I could work very comfortably with these pieces. However, my arms are heavily laden with the coal black pieces and they seem to immobilize me, so I merely continue to survey the scene.

Scattered here and there all over the table are pieces with question marks on them. They are all totally different shapes like snowflakes in a storm, not one of them the same, yet all somehow related. Some have a very large question mark drawn with a heavy hand and a broad tipped marker. Some are penciled lightly with a delicate touch. There are varied and numerous entities in between. I look at all of them over and over again. I stare at them for a long time.

In the middle of the table is an unusual piece. It is recognizably different and does not appear to be in any particular group. Although it has a characteristic difference or a seemingly distinctive quality, I cannot classify the distinction. It is attractive and pleasing to my eye and I make an attempt to reach it, but the table is too large. I walk around the table, striving to reach it but the piece remains out of my grasp. I continue to hold on to the jagged black pieces while trying to pick up the piece in the middle, which remains out of my range. This piece is God.

As I survey the puzzle of my life, I feel inadequate and not properly equipped for such a formidable undertaking. How can I possibly put these pieces together? I am actually insufficient—without enough strength or fortitude for an endeavor so toilsome and severe. My first inclination is to get the box and put the puzzle away, safely out of reach on a high shelf where I won't have to look at it. My will is weak. It seems I don't want to begin. The very thought of the puzzle box neatly tucked away brings a measure of relief. However, when I pick the box up I realize there are still more pieces left in the box!

The situation is already out of hand! And now what is left in the box, coupled with the burden of the black jagged pieces that I still cradle in my arms, is too much to bear. It is too awful. It is not fair.

I peek into the darkness of the box and it holds much emptiness. The pieces are thick looking and heavy. I don't want to dump them out. The table is already cluttered. I move them around a little with one finger, trying to get a better look but not wanting to disturb them too much. They are soggy as though they had been soaked, and in a foul solution as they have an unpleasant odor. I don't think these pieces will fit very nicely in the puzzle. Perhaps if I spilled them from the box I could better see their shapes and colors. Maybe then I might understand how they fit. But I don't want to do this. They are soiled and might contaminate the rest of my puzzle. These pieces represent my emotions.

The only other shapes I can see in the box are innumerable tiny pieces. They are covering everything like little ants climbing on an anthill. They are crystal clear in color creating quite a contrast with those other damp dark pieces. I think they are somewhat appealing and I am tempted to take them out of the box. But the problem is there are just too many. And they are also wet. They are my tears.

I place the open box on the table. Now what? I am not able to go on. And I cannot put all the pieces back in the box—the wet ones have expanded taking up all the room inside. Nothing is the same. I will never again be able to go on with life as I know it. I must somehow find the strength or will to begin anew, to work with the pieces of this puzzle, to hold the fragments still broken with sharp edges, to fondle them as a mother fondles her newborn child, and somehow nurture the shreds of existence back to life.

It is easy for me to look at the puzzle, but hard to begin. I think that growth must have occurred. Before this, it was difficult to even assess my situation, to look at the puzzle of

my life. I must want to begin . . . I must make it an act of my
will to begin to get better. It seems that everything is a
decision. As I look at the black jagged pieces of puzzle
cradled in my arm, I realize that my pain is, in essence, a part
of me, not outside of me. And awareness awakens, deep
within my heart, in my secret place. I know I must embrace
my suffering to truly be healed and to become a whole person
again.

Now, I am ready to let my tears out of the box. I have
begun to work with my puzzle.

QUESTIONS FOR REFLECTION

1. What are the pieces of your life right now?
2. What are the pieces of your pain?

ACTION

1. Write down everything that makes up the fabric of your
life right now. Include:

   ◆ people—family, friends, co-workers

   ◆ God—Where do you think he is in your life right now?

   ◆ health—nutrition, exercise, rest, your attitude toward
   life

   ◆ work—inside and outside the home

   ◆ emotions—Open the box and look at what's inside.
   (Don't worry about dealing with it right now). Identify what is hidden in there. Call it by name: anger,
   disbelief, hopelessness, guilt, despair. And what
   about the problem of tears. Are they right there just
   straining to be let out, or are they hidden deeply? Are
   they TEARS or are they tears, tears, tears, tears, tears?
   Write them all down.

2. Write down everything that causes you to feel sorrowful,
to hurt, grieve, or to feel distress. Include:

- the pain of missing your child
- the pain of remembering your child's suffering
- the pain of the funeral
- the pain of "Why my child?"
- the pain of people not understanding
- the pain of people forgetting
- the pain of powerlessness

POINTS TO PONDER

1. Healing involves the willingness to accept suffering as a part of life.
2. You must be willing to hurt more before you can hurt less.

PRAYER

They came to a place called Gethsemane, and Jesus said to his disciples, "Sit here while I pray." He took Peter, James, and John with him. Distress and anguish came over him, and he said to them, "The sorrow in my heart is so great that it almost crushes me. Stay here and keep watch."

He went a little farther on, threw himself on the ground, and prayed that, if possible, he might not have to go through that time of suffering. "Father," he prayed, "my Father! All things are possible for you. Take this cup of suffering away from me. Yet not what I want, but what you want" (Mk 14:32-36).

Jesus is acutely aware of your suffering. He understands that emotional pain can be as devastating as physical pain. He experienced authentic human emotions. He too wrestled with sorrow and suffering. He was motivated by love—love for you, me, the Father—and assisted by grace.

Slowly re-read this scripture of the agony in the garden.

Think about where you are in this picture. Walk to the place called Gethsemane with the crowd . . . some stay at the entrance . . . a few go into the garden with Jesus. It is night. Let the darkness envelop you . . . walk along a little further to where Jesus kneels in prayer . . . the night is heavy with silence and stillness. Jesus begins to experience sorrow and distress, and in his anguish he prays with greater intensity. Look at your Savior . . . he is alone. Most of his friends are not around this night . . . those who are, have fallen asleep. Only you and he remain. Begin your prayer . . . and allow your pain and anguish to surface. . . . Stay close to Jesus . . . tell him out loud how you feel. Say all the things that you would not say to anyone . . . tell him everything. Close your eyes and kneel by Jesus . . . keep him company in the garden for as long as you are able.

NINE

Faith

Faith is confident assurance concerning what we hope
for, and conviction about things we do not see.
—Hebrews 11:1(*NAB*)

The retreat house stood nestled in among the trees tucked
back from the road. An established place of peace, it had a
tendency to calm my state of mind and soothe my anxious
soul. A relaxed and comfortable feeling settled over me. It
was good to be here, and I was thankful for this weekend
away to rest and collect my thoughts. I was no longer so
heavily burdened by those harsh oppressive feelings that
took up residence with me the first year or so of grieving—
those hauntingly aching feelings that imprisoned and immobilized me in a damaging dance of despair. Since my consent
to be a bearer of pain on this walk of faith, the constraints of
persecution had been lifted.

Entering into my grief and allowing myself to feel the pain
and emptiness of the seemingly despairing circumstances

that life had dealt me—this is what in reality helped the most to set me free. The very hurt that I did not want to feel to the depths of my being was indeed the pathway to wholeness. The crucifixion always comes before the resurrection. I could now dimly see a trail through the tunnel, but I was still seeking the Light. However, I now could believe that I would one day rise up from this tangled web of hurting emotions and live life fully once again. Even though I did not have wonderful feelings to support this belief, and even though the emptiness and loss still shrouded me, with an act of my will I chose to believe that I would once again see the Lord's goodness in the land of the living. And the tiny seed of faith grew in the quietness of my heart without my realizing how this happened.

And now . . . I would have to spend some time in the tomb before the resurrection. The tomb is darkness, preventing me from sight, necessitating that I be still and know that he is God. And the tomb is damp with my tears as I continue to hold onto the black jagged pieces of pain. But the secret is still true; God does care for me, and I will have a vital life once again . . . I will awaken at peace in the morning . . . I will enjoy the sunset . . . and I will have joy once again. . . . "Blessed are they who have not seen and have believed."

Lisa was the oldest of my children. I had no experience with the pain of her separation from me. My mind continued to tease me with its hollow charades . . . "She is away at college," it suggested repeatedly. What a soothing thought— why yes, she could have been away at college. She was the right age . . . She had hoped to become a nurse and work with cancer patients. What a pleasant reverie; how good this made me feel! This harmless daydreaming couldn't hurt, I rationalized, and it produces such a favorable feeling of relief.

Many mothers I knew were enjoying these conversations. "Yes, she's away at school. We brought her there last weekend—I miss her terribly. She won't be home till Christmas." Such words from others inflicted crippling blows to my fragile state, and feelings of anger and envy reared up. In my confusion the daydream seemed so helpful;

but a small voice whispered the truth to me deep within—it is a lie . . . Lisa is not at college . . . she will not be here for Christmas. I held the black jagged pieces close to me and once again let my tears out of the box.

I continued to indulge myself in reminiscence, trying to be aware of not wishing myself in the past, but simply recalling past events from my saddened position. How well I remember my unplanned announcement of a new child to be added to our family. I had arrived home from my doctor appointment before Dennis and Lisa. They were at the medical center receiving test results that would confirm the long awaited remission. Finally, the chemotherapy was over . . . finally, the radiation was over . . . finally, we could begin to count the years of remission—each year bringing with it more positive proof of survival.

Watching Dennis' car round the corner of our street, my thoughts were on the new life growing within me. I had known this secret for months, but had chosen not to share it just yet, hugging it to myself, nurturing its tiny existence with silent affirmation of its being. Now, we could share our good news together. But as Dennis and Lisa walked toward the house, I saw that they were carrying those ugly, large, dark brown bottles, the kind that hold the isotope stuff for testing—Directions: fast for x number of hours. Drink all of the medicine before you go to bed, and don't eat or drink anything in the morning, not even water, etc., etc., etc. My mind raced about—"There must be some mistake. Our testing was over. Didn't you get the results?" I heard myself say. "No remission," announced Dennis. "It's back," cried Lisa, and she cried, and she cried, and she cried.

The months wore on—Lisa's death became more and more imminent; and the baby's birth grew closer and closer. It seemed as though I held the complete life cycle all at one time. I had a baby coming, and a baby going. As my body rapidly changed to accommodate the new life blossoming, so Lisa's body rapidly deteriorated, moving toward death . . . or life. . . . Could I say that she was moving toward life, to eternal life—through death to be born again in a new life without need of this body? This message could not quite compute. It was one thing to believe this message as a doctrine of faith, and quite another to believe this message in the form of my child's body.

My own large frame confirmed new life within, of this I was confident: yes, this baby would emerge into a life beyond the womb; and I would hold her, and touch her, and hear her cry. But my other baby, the one struggling from this womb of earth to reach life on high—where is my proof? "Faith is confident assurance concerning what I hope for, and conviction about things I do not see." Lord, are you holding that baby now? Lord, tell me this is real. Lord, I do believe, help the part of me that doesn't want to believe. All my years of religious training reverberated in my mind. Question: "Why did God make me?" Answer: "God made me to know, love, and serve him in this life, and to be happy with him in the next." The message was still in the computer of my memory, and I called this substance forth. "Yes, Lord, I do believe," I prayed, though I felt no comforting assurance. And at that moment, I named my unborn baby Grace; because with a baby coming and a baby going, we would need grace. Life and death . . . joy and sorrow . . . bittersweet . . . such is life.

"They" say that faith is holding on, hanging in there when the going gets tough. "They" also say that faith is letting go, accepting the things I cannot change. Let go and let God. I had been more familiar in my life with the "hanging on" side of faith. I didn't want to be like the "rocky ground," receiving the message gladly but as soon as trouble came, giving up. I wanted to hang on to every belief and truth that I was able to—to find a firm foothold, to dig in and hang on by the skin of my teeth till the storm passed. Now, it seemed I was having to hang on (to faith, truth, belief) and let go (of my child, future dreams, expectations for her life) at the same time . . . bittersweet again. The letting go seems harder for me.

Little "letting go's" had prepared me throughout life.

When Lisa was a tiny baby, I shared her. I handed my precious bundle into other outstretched arms, and I watched as they smiled and cooed at her. Then they gave her back to me. When she was learning how to walk, I held tightly to her chubby little hands, and with every faltering step I steadied her. Finally, of course, I let go—and she walked. But she came back to me. When she went to school I had to learn to let go for a longer period of time. She was so excited her first day of kindergarten. She didn't cling to me at all—and I wished she would. And, of course, she came back. Her first sleep over at gramma's house, first day at camp, first weekend away— and so on through life's "letting go's"—they must have all been dress rehearsals because she always came back.

And now, the final parting, this time she's not coming back. "Yes Lord, she was yours before she was mine; and it was for this that she was born, for life with you. Is this what it means to believe?" I stand at her grave now, and there is nothing to reveal a new life going on. Her body is snuggled in the womb of the world not offering any tangible evidence of eternal life on high. Her grave now looks like all the others. The grass is no longer new, and it holds its share of crabgrass and dandelions. The stone on her grave is a familiar landmark, and my heart no longer jumps into my throat when I read her name on it. I have become accustomed to this sight and my brain no longer refuses to accept this information. And God speaks through faith in my heart and asks, "Don't you trust me with her?"

Only a few weeks before Lisa died she unknowingly handed me a morsel of wisdom. She had a small collection of meaningful things on a stand beside her bed. Included in this carefully selected memorabilia was a picture of her boyfriend, the letters he had written to her, and a picture of a tear he had drawn. This latter was a skillfully drawn, many faceted, gem-like presentation of a teardrop; and in it he had written, "There is much more to a tear than meets the eye" (more wisdom from youth). This day Lisa said to me, "Mom, take all this stuff and put it in the bottom drawer of my desk."

"Oh Lisa," I replied, "are you *sure*?" She nodded her head, "He's not coming back,"—more letting go in her life, pain added to pain. He had not visited her once since she had been bedridden; no word of why. I assume he was afraid. We all were. But he was young, and he hadn't bargained for such a heavy burden when he asked a pretty girl out so many months ago. I collected her memories and put them away.

"I've been thinking, mom," she said. "People have told me that faith is believing something till it happens—kind of like, believing it so hard that it makes what you want to come true happen." I listened intently, as she spoke half to me and half to herself. With a far away look in her eyes she continued, "I think that real faith is when nothing is going right, and when you know that it will not happen the way you want it, and then you believe anyway. . . . Doesn't that sound like faith, mom?" "Yes, Lisa, that sounds like faith to me."

Yes, my baby girl, that is faith.

Yes, Lord, I will believe.

Yes, Lord, I do trust you with her.

Yes, Lord, I do trust you in her.

Yes, Lord, I do trust you through her.

Yes, Lord, I do. . . .

QUESTIONS FOR REFLECTION

1. How has your faith been shaken since your child's death?

2. What parts of your faith remain solid right now?

ACTION

1. Write down all you believed God would do for your child. Some examples might be:

    ◆ Did you believe that God would heal your child?

    ◆ Did you believe that your child would not suffer because Jesus suffered for her?

- ◆ Did you believe that there had to be a reason for your child's death?

- ◆ Did you believe that God would keep your feelings completely peaceful in grieving?

- ◆ Did you believe that faith in God guarantees a peaceful death?

2. Write down your faith beliefs as they are right now. Some examples:

   - ◆ I believe in life after death.

   - ◆ I believe that God is loving and caring for me at all times.

   - ◆ I believe that God is working in my life even if the circumstances do not look like it.

   - ◆ God wills my salvation.

POINTS TO PONDER

1. Faith is what's left when there is nothing left to hang on to.

2. Suffering is in the realm of mystery—we cannot completely understand why God allows us to suffer.

PRAYER

He went out, carrying his cross, and came to "The Place of the Skull," as it is called. (In Hebrew it is called "Golgotha.") There they crucified him; and they also crucified two other men, one on each side, with Jesus between them. Pilate wrote a notice and had it put on the cross. "Jesus of Nazareth, the king of the Jews," is what he wrote.

After the soldiers had crucified Jesus, they took his clothes and divided them into four parts, one part for each soldier.

Standing close to the cross of Jesus [was] his mother

. . . Jesus saw his mother and the disciple he loved standing there; so he said to his mother: "He is your son." Then he said to the disciple, "She is your mother." From that time the disciple took her to live in his home.

Jesus knew that by now everything had been completed; and in order to make the scripture come true, he said, "I am thirsty."

A bowl was there, full of cheap wine; so a sponge was soaked in the wine, put on a stalk of hyssop, and lifted up to his lips. Jesus drank the wine and said, "It is finished!"

Then he bowed his head and gave up his spirit (Jn 19:17-19, 23a, 25a, 26-30).

Jesus himself suffered, died, and was buried. He endured extreme physical and emotional pain. He also suffered spiritual abandonment and he cried out, "My God, my God, why have you forsaken me?" (Mk 15:34). Jesus did not die a peaceful, happy death. Crucifixion is a bloody mess. Looking at that dying man on the cross, who would have believed he was truly God . . . who would have thought that such an awful ending was really a new beginning?

As you re-read the crucifixion scripture, place yourself in the crowd and proceed to the place of the skull called Golgotha. . . . It is easy to get lost in the multitude—stay close to Jesus. . . . He is harshly treated and he willingly advances to his death. . . . Witness the crucifixion . . . and allow yourself to feel the pain and emptiness of the seemingly despairing circumstances. . . . Stand with his mother at the foot of the cross . . . she watches her child die . . . feel her deep sorrow and heartbreak . . . Remain at the foot of the cross as you begin your prayer . . . cast out all your fear and express in words what has been concealed in your heart. . . . Voice your anguish, your doubts, your confusion. . . . Bring to the foot of the cross all your suffering that has been hidden for so long . . . stay beneath the cross for as long as you are able.

TEN

Hope

If our hope in Christ is good for this life only and no more, then we deserve more pity than anyone else in all the world.

—1 Corinthians 15:19

What hopes for the future I had in Lisa. We both designed a future filled with great and wonderful things. Lisa was a planner and a dreamer, and had a full life all arranged. She often unfolded the blueprint, eager to show it to me. "After college, I'll work as a nurse and live alone for at least a year so I can see what that's like before I get married. The kids can spend some weekends with their big sister—won't that be fun? I'll come and visit all the time and you and dad will come to visit me. After I get married I'll live in a really big house and have lots of kids of my own."

She especially liked to plan her wedding although the groom's position was always vacant. "It'll definitely be the week between Christmas and New Year's. The church will be filled with poinsettias. The girls will wear red velvet and white fur muffs. Daddy and you will both cry because you will miss me so—and mom, you will be the maid of honor." "Oh no, honey, I'll be the mother of the bride." "C'mon, mom," she would insist, "you're my best friend and the bride's best friend is *always* the maid of honor." "Oh no, Lisa" (I would play my part well), "I will be a gracious and dignified mother of the bride. You'll have to choose another maid of honor." This was her favorite discussion and we would often debate the pro's and con's of mother of the bride versus maid of honor. This would always put Lisa in a cheery mood, and she'd continue further with naming her children and my grandchildren. I can picture her smiling and twirling in the kitchen, kissing me on the cheek and testing the simmering spaghetti sauce with a chunk of bread. "And I'll cook even better than this—you'll have to come to my house just to get a good meal!"

She was fun to have around and I enjoyed her teasing and dreaming. And today, I recall with deep sorrow and suffering the morning I stood on the side porch and watched the hearse depart. My thoughts shattered our hopes: "I guess I won't be the mother of the bride." My hope for the future was leaving in that hearse. So much expectation of future good was dissolved the day death arrived. No grandchildren, no wedding, no college, no high school graduation, no remission, no life. . . . The reality continues to permeate my consciousness and to sink into my being deeper and deeper as a submarine slowly descends to the depths of the sea.

When we pushed the casket down the aisle of church that day, our family huddled closely together, each touching the casket in some way and all moving it forward, leaving church as a family for the last time. Our little dark-haired seven-year-old rested her forehead on the back of the casket and sobbed loudly and forlornly, her cries speaking the language of hopelessness. Life was truly and irrevocably gone as we moved toward the completion of this ritual. The priest had spoken in his homily words of hope . . . "hope of that eternal life which God, who cannot lie, promised in endless ages past" (Ti 1:2). "O Lord, where is my 'birth unto hope'?"

Somewhere in the midst of a baby coming and a baby going, there occurred yet another birth that happened so subtly I barely became aware of its transpiring until it had already begun to grow. Only eleven days before death's arrival, I laid in the operating room awaiting the birth of baby Grace by caesarean section. All the painful preparations surrounding major surgery were as scratches on the surface of a pain too deep to approach. I lay awake and readied, waiting for the spinal anesthesia to numb my body in order that the surgically inflicted wound would not be felt. But real pain is not a guest that departs in haste; and he would linger on to welcome me to reality after the numbness had worn off.

Dennis sat by my side, clothed in hospital attire and hidden behind a face mask. His blue eyes focused on mine were colored with much pain of his own. I began to cry, a deep aching cry of helplessness. I was caught in a course of crushing events and emotions chasing each other and barreling downhill as a landslide rushes to completion unable to be halted. My doctor, a trusted friend, was affected but remained professional. "Are you all right?" he asked. A question with no answer to be sure. "I am home with Lisa," I replied "and I barely know what's going on here. Do what you have to do." And so he administered a damaging and afflictive incision, cutting deeply into living flesh in order that new life might emerge. And Grace was born, snatched from the womb amidst loud cries and protests, taken without her consent from the comfort of the only life she had known within my body. I held this tiny mortal I had named Grace so many months before, and Dennis held me, and we all three cried. The doctor continued to stitch and staple in crude imitation of mending wounds only the Master Healer could rightly repair.

Weeks after the burial, the numbing shock of death's ravaging force withdrew and the residue of pain seared its way into my consciousness and our remaining life. My eight-

year-old began to be plagued with nightmares. She screamed
and shrieked in the middle of the night thrashing in her bed.
Sometimes she awakened and sometimes not. I held her
shaking body closely, her fists clenched tightly while she
moaned and cried. Often she would awaken with a jolt,
sitting bolt upright with widened fearful eyes "She's alive,"
she screeched at me banging her fists. "She can't breath under
there. Quick we have to go get her before she suffocates."

This scene repeated itself many times. In the morning, she
didn't remember what had happened. During the day she
would often say to me, "Mommy, God raised Lazarus from
the dead and I think he will raise Lisa from the dead too."
"Oh honey," I would answer, "that will happen on the last
day." "But," she replied, "he could right now if he wanted to,
couldn't he?" With no answers, and no neighboring
theologians to summon, I fumbled along, treading unknown
paths. "If he can, why won't he?" she persisted. We never
arrived at any type of mystical explanation, and this script
continued to repeat itself, a painful incident in the sea of
many sores. This golden-haired, wide-eyed child made her
first communion that year, and received a first Bible as a gift
from an aunt. One day, we discovered and read together this
passage:

> We want you to know the truth about those who have
> died, so that you will not be sad, as are those who have
> no hope. We believe that Jesus died and rose again, and
> so we believe that God will take back with Jesus those
> who have died believing in him.
>
> What we are teaching you now is the Lord's teaching:
> we who are alive on the day the Lord comes will not go
> ahead of those who have died. There will be the shout of
> command, the archangel's voice, and the sound of God's
> trumpet, and the Lord himself will come down from
> heaven. Those who have died believing in Christ will rise
> first; then we who are living at that time will be gathered
> up along with them in the clouds to meet the Lord in the
> air. And so we will always be with the Lord. So then,
> encourage one another with these words (1 Thes 4:13-18).

And hope was born—a "birth unto hope that draws its life from the resurrection of Jesus Christ from the dead" (1 Pt 1:3, NAB).

How easily her young and innocent mind accepted this information as she experienced the spark of hope in eternal life. The hope that had been planted deep within me at the birth of Grace, like a glowing ember leapt into a flame as I listened to her account. She told the story in her own words— a broad paraphrase of scripture from an eight-year-old—as she explained to the other children at the lunch table: "First, we will hear an angel's voice and a loud trumpet. We will see the Lord himself coming on a cloud, and then Lisa's body will rise up from the ground and we will meet her in the air and all go to heaven together." She generated excitement in the younger children: "Wow! That'll be something to see!" "We'll just be able to fly up there, oh boy!" "We'll all be together again." It was an amazingly simple conversation for four small children under eight years old; and I recalled another scripture passage: "Unless you become as little children. . . ." Hope didn't make the hurt go away, but it made the burden lighter and with hope came renewed strength.

Now, it is that most dreaded time of year, the anniversary of death which overshadows all other birthdays and holidays. The seasons have already begun their tug-of-war. The warmish, fresh-smelling spring day teases its way into a still cold winter week, then flits away as quickly as it came. Soon it returns, flirting with the breeze causing the birds to chirp, and the days begin to grow longer. This is the time of year when Lisa died—a warm, sunny morning kissed with the promise of spring—but winter was still in charge and there were many bitter cold days left. My mind has begun wading through the waves of discouragement and feelings of loss that this anniversary date carries. The sea becomes turbulent once again as the waves of emotion crash down on me. But hope is a steadying anchor as I no longer lose my balance and even brave the ocean breeze. The waves of emotion no longer carry my pain because now *I* carry my pain. It is always with me. It pierces my heart like a sword causing a deep wound which is very close to my secret place that holds the truth long ago entrusted to me: God is real, and he does care for me, and I will see him face-to-face one day. I have hope in this promise in much the same way I have hope for spring to come this time of year.

I enjoy making puzzles. In my childhood my grandmother often brought a puzzle to our house when she babysat. She said that making puzzles built up patience, kind of like exercise builds up muscles. She got me hooked on puzzles at an early age; and later I got Lisa hooked on puzzles at an early age. I told her that she would gain patience. I don't know if she believed this, but we spent many an evening doing puzzles together. One of our favorites was the "kitty puzzle," a picture of a kitten walking on a piano keyboard. She loved cats and I loved the piano.

I've not worked on a puzzle since Lisa died—except the puzzle of my life. I continue to sort out the pieces in my mind frequently. It remains the same puzzle but it no longer looks so difficult to put together. All the pieces are out of the box now and the wet ones have dried some. I have been working a little with each grouping, and I can see that it will someday be put together. I am still holding the black jagged pieces. I'm not sure if I will have to hold onto them the rest of my life, but now the burden is lighter; and I know that I will be able to carry them forever, if necessary.

QUESTIONS FOR REFLECTION

1. What hopes for the future came to an end when your child died?
2. Is death really the end of everything . . . or is it the beginning of everything?

ACTION

1. Write down all the past plans or future dreams that are

no longer possible yet stay in your mind. Some examples could be:

- ◆ Did you anticipate having grandchildren?

- ◆ Were you looking forward to planning a wedding?

- ◆ Had you been planning for college? High school graduation? First day of school?

- ◆ Were you looking forward to your child's growth into adulthood?

2. Write down your hope in eternal life as you understand that to be at this time. Some thoughts on this:

- ◆ My child is with God in heaven.

- ◆ We will be together in eternity.

- ◆ There will be no more pain, no more death.

- ◆ We were created to be with God in heaven.

POINTS TO PONDER

1. God loves your child even more than you do.
2. Will you trust God with your child?

PRAYER

When it was evening, a rich man from Arimathea arrived; his name was Joseph, and he also was a disciple of Jesus. He went into the presence of Pilate and asked for the body of Jesus. Pilate gave orders for the body to be given to Joseph. So Joseph took it, wrapped it in a new linen sheet, and placed it in his own tomb, which he had just recently dug out of solid rock. Then he rolled a large stone across the entrance to the tomb and went away. Mary Magdalene and the other Mary were sitting there, facing the tomb (Mt 27:57-61).

Jesus knows that we are unable to fully comprehend his eternal plan. Our human minds do not have the capabilities to fathom the divine scope of life after death. Jesus himself, cried at his friend Lazarus' grave. Surely his mother grieved at his grave . . .

As you read the scripture passage of the burial of Jesus, position yourself near Mary, his mother. . . .

It is dusk now, and the people who had gathered have gone back home. . . .

Mary watches the men take her Son from the cross . . . is there any greater pain for a mother? . . . She holds Jesus in her arms one last time and beholds our Savior clothed in bodily death . . . it was for this he was born. . . . Watch with her as they prepare Jesus' body for burial . . . look into the tomb and see where they lay him. . . . The tomb is dark, and death is silent . . . see them roll a stone across the entrance . . . death is final, there is nothing left to do. . . .

Sit with Mary facing the tomb as you begin your prayer . . . voice your overwhelming feelings of loss and devastation . . . speak out loud to Jesus of the emptiness and despair that haunt you . . . cry out in earthly anguish the unanswered "whys" that are buried in your heart . . . empty out all the painful thoughts that lie deep within. . . . Remain sitting there, facing the tomb, for as long as you are able.

ELEVEN

Love

These three remain: faith, hope, and love; and the greatest of these is love.

—1 Corinthians 13:13

Grief is distress of mind, body, and soul causing me to feel both unlovable and unloving at the same time. In grief my mind is dulled, my thought process unclear and not functioning appropriately. I am physically worn down, unable to achieve realistic goals, and at times, even immobilized. And my soul is weary, fatigued from searching and seeking.

Lisa experienced all of these feelings in her struggle with death. I can still picture her tiny body ravaged by disease immobilized in her bed. She was unable to wash her face, move from side to side, or go to the bathroom. She could not eat or drink by herself, take a telephone call, change the TV channel. In her physically worn-down state, Lisa allowed others to help her.

One way we could show our love for her was by serving

her bodily needs. We bathed her and spoon fed her. I turned her tiny frame from side to side, and lotioned her back and legs, helped her with the bedpan, fed her ice chips. These were actions of love that Lisa permitted us to fulfill. *She let us love her.* Her mind and thought processes were not always functioning properly and she let us think for her, make decisions and suggestions. She remained agreeable, trying to spare us added pain. Her soul was wearied and fatigued from searching for answers that I don't know if she ever found. She let us pray for her and with her daily.

My struggle with grief is not unlike Lisa's struggle—only hers was with death and mine is with life. The beginning of the struggle was a severe uphill climb; and it was difficult to find the will to go on. Everything seemed to be a decision. I did not welcome the added burden of decision-making, nor did I think I was capable of making sound decisions in my debilitated state. As I entered deeper into grief, the painful hurting feelings became a way of life and I struggled to keep my balance under the heavy burden of black jagged pieces in my puzzle. I was no longer happy, smiling, witty, capable, nor did I feel lovable. This pain limited me, at times it consumed me; but I did not want to allow it to control me. I could *decide* not to act on terrible feelings.

The easiest way to do this was to share the dreadful feeling—to verbalize it to someone—this seemed to give it less power over me. With strenuous effort I fought to overcome my sense of uselessness and despair. I wanted to withdraw from people completely. In this aching, hurting state, I wanted to hide myself away, to safely shield myself from eyes and tongues that I supposed would be critical. But in effect, I did exactly the opposite. My need for comfort and support overcame the fear of rejection. Following my child's example, I let others help me. This was one of the best decisions I made in this confused condition. People wanted to serve our needs. It was their way of showing that they cared for us. Part of me wanted to tell them "Go away, leave me alone. I don't want anyone seeing me like this. I can do it myself. I don't need help." But the plain truth was I couldn't do it by myself. I did need help.

The tug-of-war raged inside me in varying degrees—not wanting people near, not wanting to be alone. People took many burdens off of my stooping shoulders heavy with their load of grief. I let them love me by caring for my needs and the needs of my family. Many cooked and brought food to the house. This support was the easiest to accept. Some people cared for my children, others pitched in and did household chores and laundry. This put me in a position that seemed unusually lowly. It was humbling. But the over-whelming feelings of sorrow and suffering quickly put my pride to flight. I was walking unknown paths and without a guide; my only companions were pain and sorrow and I did not want to journey alone.

Not being a risk-taker by personality, all my caution lights went on. What a vulnerable position I had come to occupy. It felt uneasy, uncomfortable—letting people come so close. Why, shouldn't I get myself together first, act brave in the face of difficulty, put the past behind me and go on for the sake of my other children, pull myself up by the boot straps and continue with my life? I could find no truth in any of those alternatives. The truth was I was broken and hurting, and risking rejection, I permitted other people—those who had the courage or the strength to come closer—to see the part of me I feared revealing the most, the ugly black jagged pieces.

Although my struggle still encompassed the difficulty of bearing the pain I had agreed to carry, it now took on a different dimension. The struggle also became a matter of vulnerability, openness, exposure. To allow others near me in this state was not easy, but they loved me anyway. And I began to see God's love in action. It seemed as though my human suffering, even in its silence, called forth a response of love and compassion from people. Indeed, such affliction appeared to be the very catalyst needed to move people into the gospel of caring, and it began to feel as though God himself ministered to me through my neighbors.

Somehow God's love is inexplicably linked to the mystery of human suffering in a way that cannot be reduced to mere words. Suffering puts life in perspective. My child's suffering is an indelible imprint on my mind.

I can recall every moment with clarity. It is a reel of tape I am able to replay in my innermost vision at any time. It is a program that I print out in my mind's eye at the touch of a button. Other people are also able to activate the print out. The drama still replays in the corridors of my memory. In the midst of Lisa's struggle with death, her life took on new meaning. I watched her suffering, witnessed her struggle, stood by in helplessness bearing witness to her labor with life and death. In those moments, the differences between us had long since disintegrated. The arguments had vaporized. The clashes of will had dissolved. The love within me was called forth, summoned by suffering to a new depth and breadth and length that moved beyond feelings into a different dimension. It is love that is born with pain, washed with tears, cleansed with truth, and linked to God in the mystery of human suffering. This vision of the heart, this different perspective, moves outward to other people. It is a heightened sensitivity to human suffering. It is a seedling of a new kind of love that goes beyond the ugliness of despairing emotions and recognizes hurting people with the acuity of a heart pierced with pain.

In the midst of suffering, God saw fit to bless me with Grace. Some people said of my pregnancy, "Oh no, you don't need this right now." Other people said, "This could be just what you need right now." I didn't know what I needed, but Grace was born—new life, a sign of God's love. My years of religious training remain part of the core of who I am. I can easily recall definitions of grace—a supernatural gift from God which enlightens our minds and strengthens our wills, a sharing in the life of God, a gift of God which indicates the presence of the Giver.

In hindsight, I can see that all was grace. No such journey

could be undertaken, such terrifying paths traveled, such hazardous trails covered as the valley of the shadow of death without the light of grace. As I see it now, Lisa has passed through death to life—and I remain in the valley of the shadow of death—of her death. And as I still at times journey in shadows, it seems that . . . all is grace.

Our last child, Grace, is now five years old. She is bright and mischievous, outspoken and loving. She is a marker in time. She has grown and changed, and so have I. She is learning new things about life every day, and so am I. She is a gift from God when I least expected it. She came from God and will return to him.

God's love for me is too wonderful to understand, and so much better than I gave him credit for. It goes far beyond the capabilities of my intellect. When I try to figure him out, I cannot do it. All throughout Lisa's illness when I clung to him fiercely, he had no intention of leaving me. Through the bleakness of the funeral and the numbness beyond, he stayed close to me in my broken heart, even though I did not feel it. In the bitterness and emptiness of the deepest part of grief, he was there. When I thought I had left him—I couldn't pray or read scripture; I didn't go to church; I was paralyzed in grief—he did not leave me. And still, if I run to the darkest pits of self-pity and go to the deepest extremities of discouragement, he will not forsake me. His face is always turned toward me. His love is more than I can comprehend.

From the alcoves of my faith and hopes and dreams come thoughts of my child in a new life—a life where everyone loves each other and no one is hurting. There is no sorrow, no pain, no tears. She beholds God face-to-face. She is loving me in a more perfect way than she was able to here on earth within these bodily constraints. She now has eternal vision. And she can see that in a twinkling of the eye we will all be together again.

We have given away most all of Lisa's belongings to her friends. What I held back for myself, I keep in my heart. There is a bookmark that I took from her Bible before I gave it to her friend. I laminated the bookmark in clear plastic hoping to preserve it forever. I keep it in my Bible (and also in my heart). On it is a picture of a small yellow and orange butterfly and the words, "Death begins with birth. Life begins with death—glorious fulfillment."

QUESTIONS FOR REFLECTION

1. How have you changed since your child's death?
2. What areas of your life require change for further growth to wholeness?

ACTION

1. Write down all the ways that you are different than before the death of your child. Some thoughts:

  - Are you more aware of the sufferings of others?

  - Are you less critical and more understanding of people in difficult circumstances?

  - Do you possess more courage to speak to grieving people, less fear at a wake or funeral?

  - Do you have more compassion toward others in need?

  - Do you pray more or think of God more frequently?

2. Write down the things you are aware of that could be changed. Some areas to look at are:

  - Do you in any way support other grieving people?

  - Could you choose not to act in hurtful ways even though you are hurting?

  - Do you allow people to minister to you in your need?

  - Do you need to pray more or think of God more frequently?

  - What else would you like to change?

POINTS TO PONDER

1. Love is more than a feeling, it is a commitment.
2. God's love for you and for your child is absolutely unconditional.

PRAYER

Very early on Sunday morning the women went to the tomb, carrying the spices they had prepared. They found the stone rolled away from the entrance to the tomb, so they went in; but they did not find the body of the Lord Jesus. They stood there puzzled about this, when suddenly two men in bright shining clothes stood by them. Full of fear, the women bowed down to the ground, as the men said to them, "Why are you looking among the dead for one who is alive? He is not here; he has been raised" (Lk 24:1-6).

As you slowly read this resurrection scripture, place yourself in the scene, and proceed to the tomb with the women, carrying whatever you have prepared. . . . It is near dawn and the birds are beginning to sing . . . the grass is wet with dew . . . the sky is changing from darkness to light. . . . The women walk along with heaviness and sadness . . . they do not yet realize what has happened . . . they speak softly with anguish of his death. . . . Remain silent as you walk with them . . . the morning is calm, there is a warm spring breeze . . . the conversation is laden with the shadow of death . . . but, even as they grieve, you carry some anticipation because you know what has happened. . . . Watch as they discover the stone has been removed from the entrance . . . surely now they will begin to understand . . . walk with the women into the tomb . . . they expect to confront death—but the body of Jesus is not there. . . . Surely now they will understand . . . but they are confused and fearful. . . . The angel speaks to them, "He is not here—he has been raised!"

Stand with them in the tomb as you begin your prayer . . .

the emptiness of the tomb is now bathed in light...allow yourself to feel the warmth and light . . . close your eyes and hear
the spoken word . . . he is risen from the dead. . . . Release the
weight of confusion and fear . . . Allow the light of the resurrection to enter the empty spaces in your heart.

Renew out loud your commitment to Jesus...do whatever
he tells you.

TWELVE

Prayer

When you call me, when you go to pray to me, I will listen to you. When you look for me, you will find me.
—Jeremiah 29:12-13a (*NAB*)

Prayer is raising my mind and heart to God with or without words. I can pray at a particular time of day and in a special place. I can also pray at any time and place as I go about my daily routine. It is good to do both.

The Presence of God

An effortless and natural way of praying is simply by recalling the presence of God. God is everywhere, like the air I breathe, but I don't always think about it; I tend to forget it. If air were a color, say pale pink, it would be very easy to see the air I breathe as I inhale and exhale. Whether I went in my kitchen or living room, upstairs in my house, or outside, the air would be visible. If I would go to visit a friend, to the mall, or vacationing in another state, there it would be, that pale pink air—it's everywhere. This might even cause me to appreciate it more. As it is, I take it for granted and hardly give the air a passing thought most days.

God is everywhere. As I go about my home from room to room, he is present. When I go shopping or to a friend's, he is all present, everywhere. He is in front of me, and behind me, and all around me. When I consciously bring his presence to my mind and dwell on it, if only for mere seconds or minutes, this is prayer. When I deliberately bring my mind to the realization that I am in God's presence, then I am making a decision to pray, whether or not it feels like prayer to me. When I do this frequently throughout my day, it becomes habit-forming.

This is the simplest form of prayer for me when I am in deep grief. However, it has not been easy to make this decision in the lowest valleys of grieving. My mind has not readily turned to God, as I would have liked it to. My thoughts have been riveted on Lisa and on myself and my own hurt. But when, with an act of my will, I bring my mind to realize the all-pervasive presence of God, my heart soon follows.

Repetition

A short prayer or a line of scripture repeated frequently throughout the day is a steady support. Intense grief blocks my mind from lengthy prayer; and I am unable to think of words to say. I can't even imagine what I should pray *for*; but God knows what I need. For months I appealed to God with his own promise: "You said you would *never* leave me. You said you would *always* love me." This was a prayer I repeated again and again in my mind. Sometimes I would whisper it; other times I spoke the words aloud and even shouted them when I was alone. It was a plea for assurance of his love and support in spite of the ugliness of my distraught existence. All through the day I would recapture the words in my mind and again plead with the Almighty.

The Psalms are brimming with short prayers. Some of my favorite verses are from Psalm 119:

... "My comfort in my affliction is that your promise gives me life."

... "Behold my affliction and rescue me."

... "Before dawn I come and cry out. I hope in your words."

... "Sustain me as you have promised."

So many times I balanced precariously, seemingly on the edge of sanity. With staggering steps I faltered and stumbled, fearful of losing my mind, my faith, my other children, the very meaning of life itself—and I cried out in anguish, "Holy Spirit, help me now." During these times I reminded myself, "This too shall pass." Feelings are subject to change; God is forever. Because I believe in God there is always a prayer to be said, if only "God, I do believe, help the part of me that doesn't want to believe." I usually choose only one short sentence and repeat it to myself again and again all throughout the day. I truly believe this helped save me from despair many times.

Grief as Prayer

This is a prayer of offering, when I am feeling over-whelmed with the sorrow and suffering that comes with grieving. It can be prayed with or without words. I simply open my heart to God while I am *in* grief, and I think of him while I stay *with* grief. I picture his face in my mind as I continue to go *through* my grief at this moment. I do this so much that my grief becomes my prayer—crying and weeping and mourning: "I offer this to you, O Lord. These are the ashes of what is left—this is all that I have and all that I am right now. O Lord, receive this mourning . . . I offer it to you from the inner recesses of my broken heart . . . I unite this with your suffering, O Lord, as an offering of my self." This can be prayed over and over throughout the day whenever I feel overcome by grief and discouragement. All my questioning, all my reasoning, all my lamenting is offered: "Lord, take this and accept it as my prayer, and do with it as you will."

Sometimes I visualize pictures in my mind when I pray. This helps me to accept the things I cannot change. By visualizing I am also able to put God in the picture. He's there all along. I just can't see him. A mental picture can also be a prayer support when I have no words.

The Black Jagged Pieces

This is a prayer to accept pain as a part of my life. I can picture myself holding the dark puzzle pieces that symbolize the pain in my life. I feel their shapes. They are jagged and sharp. Some are very large pieces; others are smaller. I can feel them prick my fingertips. I let them hurt me and I cry. I picture Jesus holding me as I hold the pain, and I feel his love coming to me even as I am in pain. I let my heart rise up to meet his love, and I tell him that I trust him with my child.

Circle Meditation

I am in a circle holding hands with my child and Jesus. I look at my child. I do not rush to embrace her; I simply look at her. I love her with my eyes and my heart. My child is looking at me with love, a much more perfect love than she was able to give me on earth. Slowly we both turn our faces to look at Jesus. We continue to hold hands, all three of us. Jesus looks first at my child. I watch him look at her with love; he is smiling. Then he looks at me. I can see that he loves me. We continue to hold hands.

Giving God My Anger

For this prayer, I sit on my bed and close my eyes; or I sit on my child's bed and close my eyes. I picture Jesus sitting right next to me, and I tell him I am angry. I tell him all of the ways I am angry, and how I am angry at him. He is a good listener; he does not speak. I tell him everything about why I am angry. I cry and I let him hold me while I cry.

Walking Meditation

In my mind, I picture Jesus and my child walking together in the distance. I see them from afar—they are walking slowly, looking at each other and smiling. They are holding hands and walking toward me. I watch them for a while. They are comfortable with each other. As they come closer, they both look at me and smile. They both love me and I can sense this coming from them.

Letting Go

My child and I are walking together holding hands, perhaps chatting. It is a wonderfully quiet path with tall shade trees on both sides. I see Jesus in the distance walking toward us. Slowly we both walk toward him. We meet on the path and stand facing each other. My child and I are still holding hands. I know that he wants her and he waits till I am ready. I place my child's hand in his hand. I hug and kiss her—I do not cling to her. We stand facing each other. Jesus and my child are holding hands.

Sailboat Meditation

My child is on a boat, slowly moving away from the shore. I am standing on the shoreline waving to her. I call out to her: "Goodbye . . . I love you . . . I'll miss you . . . See you soon." I say everything that I wish I would have said to her before she got on the boat—and I cry. The boat gets smaller and smaller. I can no longer see her face, but I can still see the boat. Soon, the boat is only a dot on the horizon. Then it disappears from my sight—there she goes. Jesus holds me as I cry. I tell him, "I wish she didn't have to go. This is too hard to endure." I tell him everything. He understands. But she is still in the boat sailing to her eternal destiny. I picture her on the other side, coming into view, a small dot on the horizon. "Here she comes!" The glad shout from heaven's shoreline is inaudible to my ears. They knew she was to arrive. They are waiting as the boat appears larger and larger. Finally they see her face. She is smiling and waving. Jesus is with the crowd on the shore waiting to welcome her.

QUESTIONS FOR REFLECTION

1. How has your prayer life changed since your child's death?
2. What commitment to prayer are you able to make at this time in your life?

ACTION

1. Identify and write down all the aspects of your prayer that are different than before your child's death.

   - Do you no longer praise and worship God?

   - Is your prayer a conversation with God?

   - Do you pray memorized prayers?

   - Have you blamed God in prayer?

   - Do you seek and yearn for God?

   - Are all of your prayers petitions?

   - Have you abandoned prayer?

   - Do you still in your heart have the desire to pray?

2. Put in writing the commitment to prayer that you will make at this time in your life. It may be helpful to remember:

   - A big commitment is not as good as a small commitment that you will keep.

   - If you have never made a serious commitment to prayer, start with ten minutes a day.

   - What you can do is not as important as what God can do.

♦ Include a few minutes of reading scripture, a few minutes of talking to God, and a few minutes of being quiet before God.

POINTS TO PONDER

1. "Can a mother forget her own baby and not love the child she bore? Even if a mother should forget her child, I will never forget you" (Is 49:15).
2. God desires you even more than you desire him.

PRAYER

On that same day two of Jesus' followers were going to a village named Emmaus, about seven miles from Jerusalem, and they were talking to each other about all the things that had happened. As they talked and discussed, Jesus himself drew near and walked along with them; they saw him, but somehow did not recognize him. Jesus said to them, "What are you talking about to each other, as you walk along?"

They stood still, with sad faces.

One of them, named Cleopas, asked him, "Are you the only visitor in Jerusalem who doesn't know the things that have been happening there these last few days?"

"What things?" he asked (Lk 24:13-19a).

As you re-read the scripture of the walk to Emmaus, it easily lends itself to include you. Walk along slowly with Jesus' followers. . . . You are on a tree-lined path; it is spring, breezy and warm . . . they talk and discuss events and happenings . . . you are silent and thoughtful, aware of Jesus drawing near. . . . Watch as he speaks to them and they answer . . . sense his love and concern for them . . . and for you. "What things?" he asks. As you begin your prayer, tell Jesus about the things that have been happening in your life. . . . He is not hurried, and he looks at you with such gentleness and

patience . . . you are free to say anything to him . . . you know
he will never leave you. . . . Voice your commitment to Jesus
aloud . . . continue to walk down the road in his presence for
as long as you are able.

After your prayer, throughout the remainder of the day,
consciously bring Jesus to your mind from time to time.
Believe that his presence is with you.

THIRTEEN

Help

It may now be necessary for you to be sad for a while
because of the many kinds of trials you suffer.

—1 Peter 1:6

We sat on a grassy hillside to watch the parade, lined up in
a row, my five children and I. Spring had finally won the
tug-of-war and rewarded us with a sunny, breezy, just-right
day. I felt especially light-hearted and cheerful this morning.
I enjoyed parades, and the marching bands are always my
favorite. Just the thought of forty or fifty musicians each
playing a single instrument and all blending in harmony,
gladdens my being. Watching Lisa with the band used to
warm my heart; and since her death, it has been so difficult
to even look at the high school band.

But this day, I was in complete control, that is, until the
brass section passed by me; and then grief hugged me to
himself once again and I was reduced to tears. Such a visitor
comes calling whenever he pleases without so much as a

"May I?" easily letting himself into my secret space. However, I no longer permit him to control my household as he once did. He now has to abide by my rules: he may not have any authority or leadership position, no inciting chaos permitted, and his close friend self-pity is no longer welcome to come along.

Looking back over the past years since my child died, I can identify some milestones and definite elements of help along the way. While I was grieving, I did not recognize them as being helpful, but hindsight enables me to pinpoint some things that helped me get through the grief. It's not that I still don't find myself grieving; at times, I surely do. It comes upon me quite quickly and when I least expect it. The difference is, it doesn't control me as it could in the past.

The beginning years of grief felt overwhelming—like I was walking in a blinding sandstorm with high winds and heavy sand swirling all over and around me in every direction. I was overpowered by the force of the storm and blinded by the whirling sand lashing out at me and thrashing me from all angles. I was unable to see clearly or to recognize a direction to take, subjugated to pain and confusion. Now, it seems, the eye of the storm has passed, leaving in its wake a residue of sand clinging to me from head to toe, still messy, but able to be brushed out and shaken loose.

People

Now that I am out of the center of the storm, I can see that the most important element to help me through was people. I didn't want to see them and I didn't want to talk to them, but I thank God they kept trying. I never would have made it without them. First of all, my husband was a steady support. He knows me best and loves me most. Even though he also was experiencing grief, it was in a different way. He was still able to think logically and systematically. Maybe it was the businessman in him. He just would identify the problem, look at all possible solutions, and decide on a course of action. I let him make decisions for me. I deferred to his better judgment when grief rendered me powerless. It was very easy to do if I didn't let pride get in the way. My husband was to my life what God is to my prayer. He was a rock. He was strength to me. He gave me direction.

Sometimes it was simple, such as, "Carol, you'd better go to bed early tonight. You look tired and weary." So I would. Or, "Don't do so much work but try to find a way to relax." So I would. Sometimes it was more serious direction, like the times my life seemed so cluttered that I couldn't wade through the mountain of "things to do." I made a list and asked Dennis to prioritize my list for me. He helped me to sort things out and decide what was important to do and what I could let go or put off. It was a great relief to me and such a freedom to trust my husband in this way. His strength and judgment supplied what I was lacking at that time.

I was also blessed with a close girlfriend, someone who was still there after everyone else had left. I had prayed to God and asked him to send me a friend, an easy request for the Creator of heaven and earth! All I had to do was take that extra step into vulnerability. It was well worth the risk. She cared for me even in my ugliness. I cried. She let me. I got angry. She listened. I mourned and lamented. She sat near me. She was not turned away from me by my openness, but moved to compassion and a new depth of caring. Our friendship has grown and has an added dimension of strength because of the hard times shared.

Other grieving parents or people that had experienced the death of someone close to them were helpful people with whom to talk. There is simply no substitute for someone who has "walked a mile in your shoes." They know the burden we carry for they carry it too. They know the feelings we experience for they have felt them. They are not likely to give that useless advice that people love to offer. And they are probably not afraid to talk about death. Speaking with other grieving people will also help *them* in some way.

In learning to recognize caring people, I looked for someone who was not judgmental, was a good listener, and was

slow to give advice. Some people are terrified by the depth
of sorrow that grief carries. The dark jagged pieces of pain
and anguish frighten them to the point of turning away. This
was not a personal affront to me, but a common reaction to
this unknown assailant. I knew that there *had* to be people
willing and able to bear this heavy burden. A few friends
might be able to help put the puzzle together. Others are only
able to help hold the pieces. Still others could only stand by
me while I held the pieces.

Unexpected people can be angels in disguise. One par-
ticularly difficult day when I was feeling near to despair and
struggling to simply make it through the day, my doorbell
rang. Through the curtains I recognized the piano tuner
standing on the side porch. "Maybe if I just ignore him he'll
go away," I thought. The doorbell chimed again, and yet a
third time as I struggled to think of my alternatives. Finally,
I gave in and opened the door.While he unpacked his bag of
tuning instruments, I told him of Lisa's death. He was a good
listener, and telling the story one more time eased a certain
amount of anxiety. He was an older gentleman, with a kind
and calm disposition. He spoke of the Sunday school class
he teaches and of his own journey of faith through the years.
He gave no advice. Somehow my despair took flight and I
was strengthened for the remainder of that day. I believe God
sent him to my house at that specific time. He didn't help me
to carry the dark jagged pieces, nor could he stand by me on
a long-term basis; but he let me show him the pieces. And not
only did he not reject those ugly pieces, he told me through
his sharing that those pieces were a part of life and though
it's hard, that's just the way it is.

Time

The second most important element in my journey
through grief was a decision I made early on while I was still
in shock before the full impact had hit me. I decided to take
one full year to grieve, to go through all the seasons of the
calendar without making any major decisions or big changes

in my life. I became determined not to let other people's opinions move me from this decision. I simply disregarded their expectations of me and I did the best that I could manage each day. This attitude helped toward self-preservation. People called to ask me to join different clubs and associations, especially societies dedicated to helping others. They were well-meaning and truly wanted to help, but I didn't let them rush me. I needed time to grieve; this was the most important work right now. I would truthfully answer, "I'm not ready yet."

I refused to be manipulated into guilt. I kept telling myself, "You are all right. You need this time. It's OK not to make commitments right now. Don't worry about what they think of you." This helped me avoid making demands on myself and left me free to cover the grief work. Because I was traveling in the middle of a blinding sandstorm, I didn't need to transport extra baggage. The journey was difficult enough and I was carrying the black jagged pieces. I didn't need to be responsible for excess burdens. The grief work itself is exhausting; all my reserves were needed to meet this demand. And so I merely fulfilled the duties of my state in life. I was busy enough with the basic necessities of life, and didn't evaluate anything else for at least a year.

Being Still

An important part of the whole picture has been a willingness to be still, to stop distracting myself and not yield to the impulses of the hustle-bustle of life in the fast lane. This busyness seems to give a temporary measure of relief, but in reality serves to take me away from the grief work which has to be done to get better. It may seem tempting to "keep myself busy so I don't think about things." It is hard to hurt and I don't like to feel pain, but all the busyness did not make my pain go away. It only anesthetized my thinking for a short time and delayed the process of healing. The sorrowful journey of the grief work remained after the distractions ceased.

Sometimes I used a diversion because the heaviness of grieving was so overwhelming I wanted to escape. I told myself that this was necessary and perfectly all right as long as I at least recognized that I was distracting myself temporarily because the work at hand was too difficult. Some things I used to avoid grieving: television, a quick and easy elusion requiring no effort at all; playing my piano, a wonderful get-away to another world offering much comfort; and sleep, a total escape. I put myself to bed early when I could no longer function. I don't think all distractions are detrimental. I would go to lunch with a friend and return more able to deal with life and grief. I also took a photography course at a local college; this was a planned distraction that gave me hours each week in quiet creativity.

But distractions can be harmful when used excessively to avoid facing reality. I took a lot of time to reflect, to ponder things in my heart. Don't be afraid to think about your experience with death; don't be afraid to cry. Tears are cleansing like rain refreshing the air. This crying business is difficult for other people to handle. I "observed myself" and seemed to recognize this paradox. On days when I was using every distraction imaginable to avoid looking at my feelings, people would say, "She's having a good day today." On the days I would cry and weep and mourn, people would say, "She's having a bad day today." But it seemed to me that the days I mourned were my "good days" because then I was working through grief and dealing with what has to be dealt with to get better.

Many years ago, my husband and I visited Las Vegas with a group of couples. They were anxious to experience the festivities of this city that never sleeps, built in the middle of the desert. I was anxious to see the desert. To me, it was a symbolic parallel of my spiritual life that seemed to be lived in the dryness of the desert experience. I seemed drawn to the desert longing for the experience of its unusual and strangely different type of beauty. A local priest had given us directions and also told us that the desert was in bloom this year. We were fortunate, as this does not occur every year, he said. We drove in our rented car down the glittering strip of the main street toward the emptiness beyond. We were quickly in the desert, barren wasteland as far as the eye could see, in front of us and on both sides. We could see a few low scruffy looking shrubs, and an occasional cactus, but no flowering plants. We sped on for miles and miles of the same wilderness, darkly colored sand with barely a tuft of green here and there. I wondered how many miles we had to cover before we reached the desert in bloom. Finally we decided to stop the car and walk a little. As we slowed down, tiny colorful plants became visible. When we stopped the car, to our amazement, they were blossoming everywhere. Our pace was too fast. We needed to be still to see clearly.

Changing

Change was important to me right away. To change means to make or become different. A major, significant, profound change had occurred. I did not want to tiptoe around the biggest single happening that has affected my life. I tried to start moving toward change in small ways. We switched our seats at the table and in the car. This did two things: first, we did not have to look at Lisa's empty place; second, the action spoke in silence to the whole family—change had occurred. The hardest change to make was in Lisa's bedroom. At first, we made it into a small TV room. That way we could all sit in there, which was somewhat comforting. Then the little girls kept their dolls and toys in there and we called it the doll room. Next, it became the baby's room. But we always reverted back to calling it Lisa's room or the purple room. Now, we have knocked down a wall in there and added a window, even changed the carpeting. We no longer say Lisa's room. The change is complete.

We have altered our holiday traditions. Our first Christmas without Lisa it was impossible to follow our same ways of celebrating. It was too painful. So we changed and began new traditions. We began to rebuild our life in a different way, for things will never be the same without her.

Making a Schedule

Another practical step was a simple thing that cleared up a whole lot of confusion in my life. I put myself in the routine of a daily schedule. I wrote everything down so I knew what to do and what time to do it. I wrote a list of chores for each day and how to clean my house. I focused only on one day at a time. Actually, in the beginning I had to focus on a half a day. A typical half-day schedule might read: 6:00 baby gets bottle; 7:00 get out of bed and shower; 7:30 wake up kids and get them to school by 8:30 (Martha will pick them up). Morning goal—clean kitchen before noon. 10:00 baby gets bottle. I wrote down what I would eat for breakfast, lunch, and supper, so I wouldn't have to think about it and so I wouldn't eat everything in the house.

When life got too confusing, I made a list of everything I needed to do and asked Dennis to help me number them in order of priority. It seemed to me as if I was teaching myself a course on the basic art of survival. This is what my days and nights consisted of, for a long time—basic survival.

I scheduled time to read, even if only for a short time in bed before going to sleep. It is good to read about other people's experiences with death. This helps us to relate and know that we are "normal." Our grief will always bear some resemblance to another's story of grief. The comfort comes in knowing we are not going through this alone. Many have gone before us, many will follow after us. If you read only one thing that will help you through the day and bring a measure of relief. Then it is worth it.

Reading scripture is most helpful. Even if you don't understand it, God can speak through scripture. Time to pray each day is vital to recovery. When you don't have words to say, you are still praying just by becoming aware of God's presence. God can accomplish much more than we can im-agine in a short period of time. Be gentle with yourself, and be patient. Healing will surely come because God is on your side.

Attending a seminar or retreat on grief can be a beacon of hope in the grieving process. My husband and I attended one such seminar, and had the opportunity to see ourselves in a different light. The people on this weekend were from varied backgrounds and lifestyles. They were young and old. Some had just started their grieving, and others had grown and progressed through many healing layers. Everyone had a story to share and all carried much pain. People sharing their lives gave us strength and courage to carry on, and our sharing our lives supported others in their grief. We found that we didn't have to give each other answers because we were all struggling to live without them. We were not alone and we knew we would make it through. We were also amazed at how much we had survived already.

The highlight of this weekend for me was writing a goodbye letter to Lisa. I told her how very much I loved her and missed her. It was awkward at first, but was a healing action for me to do. I explained how sad and hurt her dad and I were. I asked her to pray for us and ask God to help us. I told her all the ways that she had made me happy, and wrote about some of the sadness in our relationship. I said that I wished she hadn't died and I was angry with her for leaving me. I told her all the ways that her death was unfair to me, to our family and to the other children. I wrote about how much her life and her death would always be part of who I am. Then I said that since she was only here for seventeen years, I was glad God chose me to be her mother because I had truly loved her as much as any mother could have. Then I said that I would be willing to do it all over again because she was worth it. I ended with, "See you when I get there. Love, Mom."

Pay close attention to what your inner voice tells you. Grief work is hard enough without the added impact of a misguided inner recording. Tell yourself that you will find meaning in life again. Treat yourself as a friend. Be kind to yourself. Tell yourself that you will make it through this; that life is worth living. Remind yourself that God is very close to the brokenhearted and that he suffers with you. Say to yourself, "Never give up. God said he would always love me. God promised he would never leave me."

QUESTIONS FOR REFLECTION

1. What areas of my life do I need to take control of right now?

2. What areas of my life do I need to surrender to God?

ACTION

1. Write down the things that you are able to do to gain some control over daily living. Some steps you might consider:

   ◆ Be realistic about what you can accomplish. Use schedules and lists. Do the same thing at the same time every day.

   ◆ Realize your need to talk to people about grief. Choose someone today with whom you will share a difficult feeling. Write their name down.

   ◆ Take charge of your child's room. Spend some time in there each day cleaning and sorting. Give gifts from your child's things to others.

   ◆ Speak kindly to yourself all day today.

2. Make a list of requests for God. You might include:

   ◆ Please send me a friend to share with, and help me to trust other people more.

   ◆ Show me the ways I distract myself from the pain of grieving: food?—TV?—sleep?—busyness?

   ◆ Change my heart that I might want to begin each day anew.

◆ Give me the courage to write a letter to my child.

◆ Grant me the grace needed to never give up.

POINTS TO PONDER

1. Practical ways to help ourselves do not bring healing to grief, they merely serve to put order into our lives.
2. God alone is the Healer; all is grace.

PRAYER

One of the twelve disciples, Thomas (called the Twin), was not with them when Jesus came. So the other disciples told him, "We have seen the Lord!"

Thomas said to them, "Unless I see the scars of the nails in his hands and put my finger on those scars and my hand in his side, I will not believe."

A week later the disciples were together again indoors, and Thomas was with them. The doors were locked, but Jesus came and stood among them and said, "Peace be with you." Then he said to Thomas, "Put your finger here, and look at my hands; then reach out your hand and put it in my side. Stop your doubting, and believe!"

Thomas answered him, "My Lord and my God!" Jesus said to him, "Do you believe because you see me? How happy are those who believe without seeing me!"

In his disciples' presence Jesus performed many other miracles which are not written down in this book. But these have been written in order that you may believe that Jesus is the Messiah, the Son of God, and that through your faith in him you may have life (Jn 20:24-31).

When the disciples told Thomas they had seen the Lord, Thomas answered that he didn't believe them! These men had been close friends all throughout Jesus' public ministry. They had left everything to follow him. Together they shared

life and witnessed many miracles. And now, one does not
believe the witness of another. Jesus did not turn away from
Thomas, but he appeared to them again. And even though
the doors were locked (much like the doors to our hearts are
locked by grief), Jesus came anyway. He brought them peace
and dispelled Thomas' doubts.

Thomas' declaration of faith, "My Lord and my God!"
comes after he touches Jesus. Jesus gives us all the means
necessary to believe in him. And yet he says, "Happy are you
who believe without seeing me!" Thomas so depended on
his own capabilities that he was led astray by his feelings of
doubt. His human nature told him that seeing is believing
and feeling something makes it real. But Jesus tells him, faith
is believing without the feeling, and knowing without seeing.
Thomas, in his fear and confusion, let his circumstances
overpower his faith. But God does not change. He is the same
yesterday, today and tomorrow. God remains faithful to
Thomas, and to you.

Close your eyes as you begin your prayer . . . be aware of
the presence of Jesus in the room . . . reaffirm your faith in
him . . . declare aloud, "My Lord and my God." . . . Commit
your child to Jesus . . . tell him out loud that you believe in
him . . . tell him that you trust him with your child. . . . Thank
him for the time you had your child with you . . . thank him
for Calvary . . . thank him for the resurrection . . . thank him
for loving you. . . . Stay quietly in his presence for as long as
you are able.

FOURTEEN

Suggestions

Peace is my farewell to you, my peace is my gift to you.
—John 14:27

I offer these suggestions to you as one grieving parent to another. These things helped me. Maybe they will help you too.

1. People—the most important help in grief.

   ◆ Lean on your husband or wife, a close friend or whoever knows you best and loves you most.

   ◆ Trust other people with your feelings—tell them the truth.

   ◆ Share your grief with other grieving parents or people who have experienced the death of someone close to them.

- Find a friend. Ask God to send you a friend. Learn to recognize caring people. Look for someone who is not judgmental, is a good listener, is slow to give advice.
- Share how you feel inside with at least one other person.

2. Take a full year to grieve.
- Go through all the seasons.
- Don't make any major decisions for at least a year.
- Don't let people make you feel guilty for not feeling up.
- Disregard others' expectations of you.
- Don't let people rush you into busyness; answer truthfully, "I'm not ready yet."
- Take time to reflect. Don't be afraid to think about things that are painful.
- Cry. Don't be afraid to cry—tears are cleansing like rain refreshing the air.
- If your child has been dead for a long time, make a decision right now to take a month (or two or six), and work through unresolved grief by using these suggestions beginning with number one.

3. Be still—stop distracting yourself.
- Recognize that you are distracting yourself.
- Minor diversions can be good if they serve to renew our strength to handle the grief.
- Excessive distractions take us away from the grief work which has to be done to get better.
- Think about your experience; ponder it in your heart.

4. Change—start moving toward change.

  ◆ A major, significant, profound change has occurred; do not tiptoe around this event.

  ◆ Change the child's room.

  ◆ Change seats at the table, seats in the car.

  ◆ Change holiday traditions.

  ◆ Deal with the clothing.

5. Get a routine.

  ◆ Schedule time of day. Know what you will do with your day. Write it down.

  ◆ Make a list of chores. Be realistic—do only what is on your list. Let the rest go.

  ◆ Make a menu. List the food you will eat. Eat only what is on your list.

  ◆ Focus only on today (at first, I had to focus on half a day).

  ◆ Schedule time to read. Seek out information. Read about other people's experiences with death.

  ◆ Schedule time to pray. God can do a lot in ten minutes.

6. Write a letter to your child.

  ◆ Say everything that you wished you had said when she was alive.

  ◆ If the relationship was not right, apologize. Ask her forgiveness. Tell her you are sorry.

  ◆ Say what you would do if you could do it over.

  ◆ Tell her you love her and miss her.

  ◆ Cry as much as you can.

  ◆ Re-read the sympathy cards and letters that you received when your child died.

- Read the signature book from the funeral home.

7. *Never Give Up.*

- Tell yourself that you will make it through this.
- Tell yourself that you did the best you could at the time.
- Tell yourself to trust in God.
- Tell yourself that your child loves you.
- Tell yourself that these painful feelings will lessen—this too shall pass.
- Tell yourself—never give up. You can make it. You can do it.
- Tell yourself that you will again have joy and peace.
- Tell yourself that you will rebuild your life.

Epilogue

There are many questions . . .
There are no answers . . .

— How do you mend a broken heart?

— Why did my child have to suffer?

— Why does God permit suffering?

— Why did my child die so young?

— Why was my child robbed of life?

— How does Death choose?

— Why is God so silent?

— Does it hurt God to see us suffer?

— Why does God seem to withdraw when I need him
the most?

— Will I ever be a whole person again?

— Will I always have a missing piece?

— If death is the passage to our eternal reward, why
does no one want it?

WHEN A CHILD DIES

— Why is it so hard to go on living?

— Why do people avoid mentioning my child's name?

— Is death really the greatest healing?

— Why are some people healed and not others?

— What is it like being dead?

— What did my child feel in that first moment of eternity?

— Can my child be truly happy in another life seeing me so sad here?

— If my child could return to this life, would she want to?

— What does her body look like now?

— What does she look like in eternity?

— What will she look like when I see her again?

— Can she see me?

— Does she watch over our family?

— Will my other children remember her?

— Why do people assume I have "gotten over it by now"?

— Why does it hurt so much to love?

— Will the hurting ever stop?